Practically Perfect Wedding and Commitment Ceremonies:
your guide to finding the right words

Rev. Angel Booth

Who needs this book?

Imagine the perfect wedding or commitment ceremony. Yours. Your perfect ceremony reflects your beliefs, your commitment and your style. If you can create the ceremony you want, one that speaks for you and includes you, within the church or temple where you attend or in which you were raised, you probably do not need this book. The church and temple have their own ceremonies and protocols for the preparation and delivery of every event.

You need this book if—

your church does not speak for you,

you are "not really religious," or non-religious; non-spiritual but developing a personal spirituality,

you have a better sense of what you are *not* than of what you are,

you imagine your perfect ceremony unfolding in the backyard, on the beach, or in a ballroom, and you can't get your minister to come to you,

you need help discovering and compiling the right words for the perfect celebration of your love.

You really need this book if you want to write your own ceremony, but don't know where to begin.

Begin with this book.

"Our contemporary culture has largely shifted from the group practice of religion to the deeply intimate search for an individual spiritual path."

— Carolyn Myss, *Sacred Contracts*

Table of Contents

Foreword

Let me tell you before you hear it on Oprah: I am not married. Yes, I have married and divorced twice. And, I still believe in marriage. I would make the commitment again.

My mother said we were raised 'backsliding' Episcopalians because we seldom went to church, though valiant efforts to do so were made on a weekly basis. In the church of my family, marriage is to be "entered into reverently, discreetly, advisedly, and soberly, and in the fear of God." I do not wholly disagree with church dictum, growing into accord with it just took most of my life.

My first husband, Tony, and I approached the state of holy matrimony feverishly, romantically, and before it was over, near-hysterically, and in the fear of our families. We were 21 and 20 at the time, and we wanted to do everything right. Our families fanned and sighed through the longest marriage service they or we had ever heard of, on the hottest day in recent memory for Northern Virginia. We even took communion, swaying occasionally and sweating through our formal wear.

After our wedding, we rarely went to church, preferring instead a holy communion with catfish on the upper Potomac River. We were best friends.

Four years downriver we were in trouble. We seemed to be outgrowing each other, or growing in different directions. We moved to San Francisco to break new ground, stimulate newness in our marriage and revitalize our lives. Instead, we grew further, and then fell completely, apart.

We left the Do-It-Yourself Divorce center hand-in-hand, genuinely relieved and happy. We assured each other that we would not wreak havoc or bring harm through a nasty divorce or custody battle for our daughter. To prove it, we fought more in that first year apart than we had our whole 6-year marriage.

Then, for our daughter's sake, we decided we could be civil. Civil led to friendly, which eventually allowed us to be friends again—and now we are family. Our daughter, now 32, had to grow up with us.

John, my second husband, was the polar opposite to Tony. He was 10 years older than me, professionally established and he seemed to always know his own mind and live on his own terms. We lived together for 5 years before we made the short trip to City Hall. Tony was one of our witnesses.

Our only reason for marrying was to better our financial position in order to refinance the house we were remodeling. We had no need of marriage for its own sake. Lacking any true foundation, our marriage, and our "living arrangement" fell apart in less than a year. By the time our divorce was finalized, I had completed seminary and become a minister.

I now believe that the causes for our partings, like the reasons we come together in the first place, have to do with the nature of our personal spiritual evolution, our contracts with each other and with God. I am grateful for all I have learned through my marriages and friendships. I remain open, expectant for the next "soul mate" to arrive and our relationship to unfold.

When performing a marriage ceremony, I feel like Merlin casting a spell. At the conclusion of this spell, people are more in love than they were moments ago; happier than they've ever been; united, joyous and celebrating. Their families and friends form a community, which wraps itself around the couple, gaining its energy, identity and purpose from the joining of these two souls. And I get to say the magic words.

Weddings inspire us and uplift our relationship values. Oftentimes, especially over champagne, a couple's community let their collective hair down about marriage, commitments, sexuality, family, culture and the challenges of blending families. I've enjoyed many deep spiritual discussions with people I've just met.

Ceremonies make way for culture to be fully present and proud, 'out' in every conversation. Before the ceremony people introduce themselves as lawyers, artists, accountants. By reception time they have been magically re-awakened into Poles and Brazilians, Filipinos and Lebanese. Here, the Midwestern part of the clan; there, the Southern or The Bronx contingent.

Family elders give us the longer view of community through their history and experience. They introduce the younger generation to the customs of their parents and grandparents. They deepen our appreciation and remind us of the slender threads that bring us and bind us together.

We toast to everything wholesome. We treat our senses to familiar and strange sights, sounds and flavors. Kids fight over flowers and ribbons and run circles around parents, 'counting coup' on all adult seriousness and decorum. The girls try to preserve the perfect-ness of their dresses and hair; the boys try not to. We all try to look and act our best. We usually end up just being ourselves.

Each community takes on a life of its own—growing from occasion to occasion. Sometimes I am invited back into a community to perform another marriage or a baptism, as new members come into the fold. Or a memorial when someone leaves. It is gratifying to be a part of the life and flow of these communities founded in love.

I am grateful to those couples exercising the audacity to arrange a wedding or commitment ceremony (or a baptism, dedication, house cleansing, business blessing, for that matter), which calls together people who care, suspends us in time and marks our lives with a special occasion.

It would be so easy to slip off to Las Vegas or the local JP to make it official. Millions of people just skip the ceremony and continue the living together as if no change of pace were necessary.

I love that some will stop, reflect and shift consciousness by gearing down into the present moment. I love that some will bravely and openly declare their love and intentions in an age where it's often more tempting to hide out than to be out about who you are.

You courageous lovers do us a great service: you direct our attention to what matters most, you bring our personalities together for a breath of fresh air, drag our spiritual beliefs out into the light of conscious awareness. Your ceremonies lift our appreciation for each other out of the doldrums of daily relating, renewing our faith in relationship. Not the least of which, you give us something wonderful to look forward to and something sweet to remember.

Acknowledgements

Grateful acknowledgment is made to the following for permission to reprint previously published material:

Carolyn Myss: Excerpt from *Sacred Contracts: Awakening your Divine Potential*, Carolyn Myss, 2002, Three Rivers Press, New York, with kind permission from the author

William Zinsser: Excerpt from *On Writing Well*, by William Zinsser, Copyright 1976, 1980, 1985, 1988, 1990, 1994, 1998 by William K. Zinsser. Excerpt from Chapter 3, "Clutter" from *On Writing Well*, Sixth Edition published by Harper Collins

The Prophet by Kahlil Gibran, copyright 1923 by Kahlil Gibran and renewed 1951 by Administrators C.T.A. of Kahlil Gibran Estate and Mary G. Gibran. Used by permission of Alfred A. Knopf, a division of Random House, Inc.

"What Marries Us?" from sidebar, Ch. 1 from *Weddings by Design* by Richard Leviton, Copyright 1993 by Richard Leviton. Reprinted by permission of HarperCollins Publishers, Inc.

Excerpt from *The Book of Psalms: Selected and Adapted from the Hebrew* by Stephen Mitchell, Copyright Stephen Mitchell, by permission from HarperCollins Publishers, Inc.

"Church of Natural Grace Wedding Ceremony" and excerpts, courtesy of Church of Natural Grace/Psychic Horizons, San Francisco, Laura Hopper, Director

"Reflections on Marriage" excerpt from *Weddings from the Heart* by Daphne Rose Kingma, Copyright 1991, 1995 by Daphne Rose Kingma, reprinted by permission of Conari Press, Berkeley, California

Excerpt from *Notes on Love and Courage* by Hugh Prather, Copyright by Hugh Prather, 1977, Main Street Books, Bantam Dell Publishing Group

Anointing ritual excerpted by kind permission of the author, Z. Budapest, from *The Holy Book of Women's Mysteries* by Z Budapest, 1989, Wingbow Press, Berkeley, California

"Song" by Allen Ginsberg, *Collected Poems 1947-1980*, Copyright 1984 by Allen Ginsberg, HarperPerrenial, Harper & Row, NY

Excerpts from *New Revised Standard Version Bible*, Copyright 1989, by the Division of Christian Education of the National Council of the Churches of Christ, Published by Thomas Nelson, Inc., Nashville, Tennessee

How to use this book

Practically Perfect is a how-to book for writing or compiling your own wedding or commitment ceremony.

About Part 1

We begin your quest for the perfect words and rituals as we would approach building a house. We begin with a solid foundation. The foundation for the life you build within, and the life you build with another, is Belief. Decisions, values and priorities are founded on beliefs.

Chapter 1 can assist you to uncover the foundation of belief you already have within you and find the congruencies of belief with your mate.

Chapter 2 will assist you with another crucial building element: having a plan. Plan for life after the ceremony!

Chapter 3 will provide ideas for gathering and organizing your thoughts about the ceremony itself.

You probably know yourself pretty well to be approaching this level of commitment with another person. You may know your beliefs and values, and have a plan in mind for the ceremony and your life beyond it. I encourage you to read the first two chapters anyway. You may find some thought provoking questions and phrases to help you think more deeply about your partner's perspective and the possibilities for the future of your relationship.

About Part 2

Discover how a ceremony is constructed, take one apart and consider the intention behind each part.

Decide which parts and complementary elements to include in your ceremony.

Define qualities that personalize your statements and vows; great tips on writing your own!

About Part 3

Select the words, phrases and statements that best speak for you.

Personalize your ceremony with beautiful poems and prose. You'll find some suggestions for how and where to include them.

Perfect your ceremony with just the right ritual. The section called "Civil Rites and Rituals" will help you find the perfect little extra something to make your ceremony special and memorable.

Gratitude

To courageous couples who step forward with hope and trust,

To all the couples and their families who invite me into their lives,

To Church of Natural Grace and it's daring mission,

To Mother Ocean, Father Sun and Sister Moon, your constant presence and permission; for friends who read this book and gave time and valuable feedback; for couples who worked this book into better form; for all the couples wed, blessings flowed, the stories told and still unfolding,

I thank you.

Special Thanks

To Rose-who-knows-I-can, and Bruce, Michelle and Judy for compassion in truth; to the bulldog of the Web; to Sheila for voice lessons, the first good draft and for Melton . . .

For Julian

Part 1

Personal Preparation

Chapter 1

Begin with Belief

"What Marries Us?"

You are about to give yourself completely to the journey of a living union. In this age of multiple choice answers to life questions, marriage and life partnership, though the most rewarding, are the least easy options. I believe in marriage. I believe in what we try to achieve through marriage—to live in harmony and loving cooperation with one other human being.

Planning and constructing your ceremony may put harmony and cooperation to its first major test. When it gets down to selecting the words and rituals you may discover your partner has a very different "God-view."

The Essential Question

From a church perspective, Marriage is a holy union, not to be taken lightly; a journey, "a state of being, to be entered into advisedly, soberly and reverently . . ."*

As you approach your new level of commitment, I encourage you to settle some essential questions about your most essential belief. Question yourself, and be open to questions from your partner and your officiator on matters of spirit, belief and intention. Dig underneath these questions with curiosity and wonder. Soberly consider your marriage and reverently prepare yourself for your wedding. Your holy union is not only with each other—it is with God.

So, what if you don't believe in God? Well, what *do* you believe? Or, as Richard Leviton put it, beyond the modern legal and social conventions,

*"What marries us?"***

You may first want to make a distinction between what you don't want to believe (or no longer believe in, such as the god of your youth or your parents) and what you do believe. Then as you clarify your beliefs, work to communicate those beliefs to yourself and your partner. What you believe forms the foundation of your thoughts, judgments and tolerances. What you believe is displayed in your life choices, and will continue to influence your future, your children, and the quality of life you live.

Belief in something 'greater than self' is what enables you to think in possibilities. Because your beliefs frame your every perception, what you **believe in** becomes the ground of your self-concept. Your ceremony will feel just right when the 'right words' perfectly reflect what you believe. How do we come to be here with consciousness and feeling? Beyond the physical level, what created us?

I urge you to stretch your mind, your vocabulary and your feelings to identify your most essential belief. Without a deeper definition and personal connection, non-belief in God is insufficient; mere belief in God is insubstantial.

---

* *The Book of Common Prayer of the Protestant Episcopal Church of the United States of America; the form of Solemnization of Matrimony*

** *"What Marries Us" borrowed from Richard Leviton's essay on belief from his book, Weddings by Design: A guide to the non-traditional ceremony 1993, Harper San Francisco/Harper Collins Publishers*

After some careful questioning,
Darcie and Darryl were able to come to an understanding that would enable them to find the right words and rituals for their marriage ceremony. Darcie does not believe in God, or in one all-powerful being, up there, ruling the universe. Darryl believes in a Great Spirit or Energy of which we all are a part, all contributing to universal consciousness. Darcie did not want the word "God" in the ceremony text, but would concede to "spirit" and even "divine" for Darryl's sake. She does acknowledge a guiding and organizing principle, or energy, at work in the universe. But it is not an entity and she thinks it operates more closely to the laws of physics than the tenets of religion. To help create their ceremony, I need to know: Does that same organizing energy reside in her, work through her? Yes? Ah, we have found a common language for divinity.

Prepare Yourself!

Before your families bear down upon you with questions and concerns about everything from your choice of officiant to your mortal soul, know your own heart and mind. It may take a lifetime to fully answer the following questions. Some would say there is no more noble pursuit.

Ask Yourself:

What gives life? Is it God, a Supreme Being, a SupraConsciousness, a Creator?

You determine many of the events of your life by the choices you make, but what guides the unfolding of those events in space/time? What energy or principle organizes nature?

Are you part of it?

What shall we call it? How would you incorporate your beliefs into your ceremony?

What marries you?

Advanced Curriculum for Lovers: Tuning In

Ask Yourself:

What does my partner believe about religion?
Spirit? Soul? Death? Birth? Re-incarnation?

Do I hear his/her truth?

Do I relate?

Describe to your partner your understanding of her beliefs. Ask more questions and keep reflecting back what you hear until *you know that your partner knows that you know what she believes.*

In addition…

Most essential beliefs and life values are formed within our family of origin. We first gain a spiritual perspective by direct and indirect contact with the god (or lack thereof) of the family. As we develop our own perspective, we will gradually separate from our spiritual upbringings. In much the same way we move away from the family home and values in order to give shape to our own. Moving away symbolizes adulthood and self-sufficiency, defining our own values, finding our place. The origins of the bachelor party the night before his wedding symbolizes the groom's departure from his mother's home and the transition to a home he makes with his wife.

We separate ourselves from our parents' sense of truth in order to discover our own. We begin to rebel or push against their moral foundation in early teens, and though it may take several years, are meant to complete the process as we physically move away to our own home or go off to college.   If we stay in the rebellion process, we do not mature. Rather, we form a habit of judgment that enables us to reject people, experiences and information in order to slow our own rate of growth.

Maturing happens as we begin to soften our repulsion to others' beliefs and values, let them be, and focus on discovering, defining and ordering our own. Our lives truly begin as we move toward our life and personal center more than we move away from other centers. We build a fulfilling life by moving toward what we want.

In her work on healing, Carolyn Myss suggests our families teach us about survival but not evolution.*** Your family can only take you to the shores of their own land. You must sail into the realms of what you will know and need to know under your own steam. It may require the rest of your life to define what is true for you. Discovering this truth will take you into your own heart. Waste no time blaming outside forces for what is not true for you. Seek instead the knowledge and mysteries of your inner experience. Develop a deeper, more respectful relationship with yourself, and your god, and bring your whole self into your marriage.

*** *For more complete information on this topic, explore Carolyn Myss' Why People Don't Heal*

Chapter 2:

Principles for Living and Relating

Beliefs determine Values

Values define what you believe to be true, and what is important to you. You will act out of your personal values when selecting the right words, a minister, the ceremony environment, and the style of ceremony. The words spoken will reflect your beliefs about marriage and your relationship—as you see it now, and as you see it developing in the future. Understanding your values first will enable you to negotiate with your partner for the elements that are important to you. Knowing your values will help you handle conflicts and key decisions during the planning and creation of your ceremony. A memorable, personalized ceremony will flow from your collective values and beliefs.

The following exercises for defining and communicating values will help you see your beliefs more clearly. The listening exercise and guidelines for discussion will help you listen more carefully to the beliefs underlying your partner's values. To clarify your perspective on marriage and commitment, take time to think about and write about the following three principles: 1. Values become behavior, 2. Devotion is commitment in action and 3. Provide and Protect (being responsible)

Principle 1

Values Become Behavior

Values Exercised: Self Knowledge, Clarity, Intimacy

Discover: 5 to 10 minutes alone

Stop now and make a list of ten top values, ten personal qualities that you consider important to every relationship. (Examples: commitment, sharing, love, forgiveness . . .)

Circle the top three to five personal values.

Reflect upon each top value, and write a sentence for each that describes, in simple terms, why that value is important to you.

Share: 5 to 10 minutes each

Discuss with your partner your top 3 to 5 values, why they are important to you, and what the living of these values might mean to a healthy relationship.

Listen carefully to your partner describe his/her top 3 to 5 values, why they are important to him or her, and what the living of these values might mean to a healthy relationship.

Apply: 5 to 10 minutes together

Reflect together on how your individual and shared values can best be served and expressed in the ceremony style (formal, casual, traditional, radical), location, time of day, ideas to be conveyed, etc.

Discussion Guidelines:

Listen carefully without judging each other's values and the prioritizing of those values.

Listen without interrupting each other.

Pose a careful question or two in order to get a clear understanding.

Use "I" statements to avoid sermonizing (Example: "It is most important to me that I be honest in communication . . ." instead of, "You should communicate honestly . . ." or "everyone needs to communicate . . .")

Remember that most conflicts in relationships arise from the perceived differences in our personal values, or the ways in which we prioritize them. To really understand your partner, it is important to let him express his values without fear of judgment from you.

Intimacy=Into-Me-You-See

Principle 2

Devotion is commitment in action

Be devoted to yourself, to each other, and to the concept of marriage or committed relationship. Devotion energizes your commitment.

Devotion is expressed in the time you give to yourself: do your homework—look at your values and priorities and what they are based upon. Be willing to grow and learn.

Devotion is also expressed through what you give to each other: permission for differences, time and energy to listen, time to plan and create together, and time to be apart.

Commitment to the relationship or marriage also means that you **uphold the relationship** when in conflict. Remember, conflicts are about different values and perspectives. If you can talk (or fight) about values, you create opportunity to reach understanding without injury to each other. If you take a swing at the marriage itself, you may undermine the certainty and trust you are building, and that may be very difficult to repair.

On a 1-5 scale, 5 being brilliant, how devoted am I to my own growth?

How devoted would my partner think I am
to the success of our relationship?

Have I felt a threat to my relationship enter into an argument?

Is there any unfinished business that my partner
and I can clear up before our wedding?

Will I?

Principle 3

Provide and Protect

Take personal responsibility for the energy you bring to the relationship.

Provide spaciousness and respect for each other as spirit and personality, each with your own life path. Remind yourself that you and your partner *chose* to create a common path.

Provide a safety net for each other by sharing your thoughts and feelings, as well as decisions and responsibilities.

Provide each other with a safe, calm home environment.

Provide growing space by *being* an environment that allows for questions, discoveries, failings and a wide assortment of emotional experiences.

Protect each other's privacy and the sanctity of the relationship. Become the guardian of each other's freedom and solitude.

Protect your home environment from pollutants of negative people and influences.

Protect your respect for each other through conscious edification. To edify means to build up. Build up your partner's sense of self worth through thank-yous and pleases, compliments, and by being your partners' best friend.

Protect trust by avoiding character assaults, name-calling and language that blames or shames.

Fight Fair: Argue about the issue, not about the person.

Defend your partner when he or she is absent. Do not allow negative comments or gossip to tear down what you are building.

Ask Yourself:

(A few minutes every day)

How do I provide for the long-term success of my marriage?

What else can I "bring to the table?"

How do I protect my own integrity?

Advanced Curriculum for Lovers: Why Are We Here?

Philosopher and Spiritual Teacher, Ram Dass, encourages us to think of ourselves as spirit having a human experience, not the other way 'round. To think of yourself as spirit, call yourself up and out of your personality, and out of your ego, the part of you that takes it all so seriously. As spirit, you are already all that you aspire to be—you are fully capable.

Ask Yourself:

From the perspective of spirit, why am I having this particular human experience—why am I here, becoming a conscious human being?

What work do I have to do in this lifetime?

What part of that work is being done through relationship?

Chapter 3

Getting the picture

Participation

The following pre-planning exercises are suggestions for getting a clear picture of the wedding or commitment ceremony that's right for you. If you are both ready to move ahead, go directly to the exercises. If you are reading this alone, stop right now. Have the reluctant or absent partner read this page.

If you, or your partner, are prone to saying, "Yeah, that sounds OK" or "I don't care. You decide." Beware. Somewhere during the planning or ceremony you will care. Better to do a little discovery now, daydream a little, brainstorm a bit. You may find out what is important to you. If, after some discussion, you decide to turn over most or all major decisions to your partner, you will know you can trust them to make the right decisions, and you will be a better support to your partner in planning and moving ahead.

Watch your language!

What I have heard:

"He/she is the creative one."

"I don't know about this stuff, he/she is better at this stuff."

"It's fine with me—whatever you want."

"I don't have time."

"He (she) is the one who wanted a ceremony . . ."

What it sounds like:

"I don't care."

"I don't want any responsibility."

"I don't want to do this."

"I don't know what I want."

"It doesn't really matter."

Avoid misunderstanding and hurt by getting clear about what you want and communicating your needs to your partner. Do not assume he or she knows enough to decide everything for you. Take personal responsibility for what you are creating together.

Pre-Planning Exercises

Set aside a day, or a weekend, for pre-planning. You will not need all of that time for focused discussion. The idea is to give you enough time to relax, with no immediate agendas, no interruptions, no hurrying to get somewhere. Sometimes you have to soak the beans overnight!

Brainstorming

Allow an hour or more. Have paper and pens, or flip chart and colored markers handy. Share your ideas, images, wants, don't wants—just blurt out ideas as they come to you. Write the essence of these ideas in one or two words somewhere on the paper. "What kind of ceremony shall we have?"

Brainstorming Guidelines:

Avoid neatness! Doodle, color, jump around the page

No idea is too crazy, too outrageous, or too dumb to blurt and write

Make mind maps, or just record ideas in a random fashion

Have fun! Keep it light. Allow ideas to pop like popcorn, or flow into each other, or build on each other.

Later, you can glean little treasures from these randomly recorded thoughts and ideas. Important and creative decisions may hatch from this mind game.

Collage Making

Allow 1-2 hours. You will need a pile of periodicals (re: bride, wedding, travel, home magazines), two scissors, two glue sticks, 1 or 2 large poster boards, or a large piece of cardboard (3'x3'), or equal amount of butcher paper (optional: a bottle of good wine, 2 glasses and your favorite background music).

• Flip through the magazines, cut out any images that appeal to you.

• Don't focus too closely on the task, just snip and chat and have fun.

• Use the glue sticks to not-too-carefully create a collage of images that appeal to you.

• Talk about your choices. Some may even relate to your ceremony.

Decisions Bill's biggest decision was to let Sherry decide. He deferred to her judgment about the location and the officiator. She chose the colors, the caterers and photographer. Bill left it all to Sherry. Then he complained about some of the people she invited, the expense of the hall she rented. He hated the DJ she hired; she should have hired musicians. His mother and sisters were not included in some of the planning, and he criticized Sherry for leaving them out of the ceremony. Sherry felt set up for failure. She was angry with Bill and approached the wedding ceremony worried about what else could go wrong.

Time Alone

Allow an hour or more. Take a walk alone or take some uninterrupted time for yourself. You may want a note pad and pencil. The task is to use your imagination and memory to get some clear ideas of what you want your ceremony to be, or not be.

Explore your memory: Select a memorable wedding or other ceremony that you attended or read about, saw in a movie, etc. What did you like about that event, what didn't you like? What was perfect, and perfectly horrible, about that ceremony? How did you feel at the time?

Explore your senses: What do you want to see in your ceremony? How do you want to feel? What smells, sounds and other sense qualities come to you? Who is there to celebrate with you? How do they feel? How would you like them to feel?

Imagine you are overhearing your best friend describe your ceremony to someone else. What kind of experience did he/she have?

Explore your values: What aspects of ceremony and celebration do you feel strongest about? What about Family, Location, Live music, Participants, Style or size of event? Where are you able to negotiate? Can kids attend? Catered food? Indoor/outdoor event? In a church or rented hall?

Note: Pay attention to what is not negotiable.

Perhaps you strongly feel that this should be a solemn event, or *not*. Or, you need to include or omit "God" in the text. Is there a member of the family who absolutely will, or will not, be invited? It is important to know your 'absolutes' so you can decide together how to create a ceremony that reflects both sets of values.

Consider what you have written or described to yourself. Notice the values being expressed through what you want or don't want—even the negatives can bring something positive to the surface.

Note: Put your thoughts into a positive frame.

For example, if you are dead set against a large wedding, no more than 50 guests—ask yourself, why? By thinking more deeply, you may discover the positive "frame" or value is about intimacy or privacy. So, when the time comes to share these ideas with your partner you could say, "It's important to me that our ceremony feels intimate and sacred. How could we arrange it so . . ." or, "I'd love to share this event with our family and our very best friends. Can we limit the invitations to 50?"

Positive phrasing, or framing, will allow your partner to hear what's true for you, and what is important from your perspective. You will find ways to negotiate without losing your essential value.

By the way: Several couples I have married or confirmed in their commitment have opted for small or private ceremonies followed by huge receptions or parties at a later

date. Many have family on the East coast or in Hawaii, Europe or Asia. Extended family was spared the expense of travel and the couples looked forward to future exotic celebrations in their honor!

Time Together

After you have invested time with yourself to discover your values and needs for your ceremony, set aside about two hours to share with each other. Remember the exercise about sharing values? The rules for discussion are the same. Before you begin, agree to listen without judgment.

Paint 'word pictures' for each other. Remember, the details will emerge from the picture you are creating together. With positive framing, share what you want to see, how you want to feel, how you want your ceremony to be remembered.

Imagine together how you will describe your ceremony 10 years from now to your kids or your friends. You may want to tape record your discussions to minimize the distraction of scribing notes.

When you feel you have reached a general agreement about what the ceremony means, and how it will flow and feel, you are ready to hammer out the details. And, now that you have done your homework, listened carefully to each other and found accord, the "right words" should fairly leap off the page when you see them.

Negotiating Values *Kelly and Suzuko wanted to have a private, intimate ceremony. Both families pressured to have a big celebration. The couple decided to honor everyone's needs. The guests assembled inside the restaurant where Suzuko had planned a wonderful celebration. Kelly, Suzuko, their witnesses and I walked out to the end of a small pier next to the restaurant. The fishermen stood aside for about 10 minutes while we conducted a brief, private ceremony. Family and friends watched from the restaurant windows.*

Chapter 4

A Planning Sketch

Who, What, When, Where, How

The really organized couples keep a binder! There are many wedding books with terrific workbook-style planning pages to help you keep track of florists and caterers and musicians and such. This is not that kind of book. My experience lies in the ceremony itself.

The following list is based on the questions I ask couples about their ceremonies. The items tagged with ** indicate the need for more detailed information from me, or more thought from you. I have fleshed out these items in the ****More About**** section, following the planning sketch.

Your Planning Worksheet

Your officiator may want to know . . .

Celebrants
full names, address(es),
day, evening and
cell phone numbers

Ceremony Date/Time
day or night

Location
Ceremony address,
phone and contact person

Reception address,
phone and contact person

Courtyard, backyard, gazebo, garden?

Directions
Provide maps
(Especially for out of town ceremonies)

Celebrant's parents
full names (if attending)

Attendants Names
Maid/Matron of Honor or Attendant

Best Man or Attendant

Other Attendants

Flower bearer

Ring Bearer

Number of Guests
Ceremony
Reception/celebration

Ceremony Staging
I ask, "So, what's it going to look like?"
Then I just listen and make notes as you
take turns painting word pictures for me.
What will happen first? Next?

Commencement
Who will cue the music, celebrants or
wedding party? How will they cue? **

Children
If children are involved in the ceremony,
who will be in charge *for* them? **

Special readings,
Who will do what, when? **

Exchanges, rituals
(for placement within the ceremony.
see Part 3)

Special colors, Props, or other details
Wine glass, circle of flower petals, or
ribbon for hand-fasting . . . have a plan
for getting it done. For example, if you
want to include a wine ceremony: Will
there be an open bottle or just a glass of
wine? Will there be a small table to hold
the wine until we arrive at that part of the
ceremony? Who will make sure the wine
will be on the table?

Special requirements for the officiant
Includes date and time for rehearsal, arrival
time for the ceremony, what to wear, and
other expectations**
I often wear a white robe and Guatemalan
priest's stole. I am happy to wear the "blue
suit" but I have found that most couples
want the more official look.

Wedding License When and where will
we complete the process by signing and
witnessing the license? **

Your minister/officiator may also want
to know about your essential beliefs and
values. What kind of ceremony do you
want to have, what feeling-tone do you
wish to convey? And, why do you want to
get married?

More About

Communication

As a minister, I need to know that you really do have it covered. I don't need to be in charge of the details, just informed about them.

Controls

Who is in charge of the ceremony? Will you have a wedding or ceremony planner?

Some wedding sites (hotels, inns, wineries) have wedding planners on staff or on-call. You may not have an option whether or not to use them. For instance, the wedding planner or coordinator will act as liaison between hotel, food service and wedding party, so the hotel will be able to function in their role without confusion. Most coordinators will also be on hand to guide the rehearsal.

If your wedding or event planner is going to run the rehearsal and cue the ceremony, let your officiator know in advance. If you do not have a planner, ask your officiator. He or she should be able to lead the rehearsal.

Christine and Phil put the ceremony site, set-up, rehearsal, reception and dinner, food and drinks into the able hands of the event coordinator at Madronna Manor here in Northern California. Chris and Phil and I coordinated the actual ceremony, with minimal input from me. They knew what they wanted. They were clear about their expectations. They were completely relaxed (well, Phil was a little nervous about getting married) and in charge. The whole event was fun, satisfying for all, technically seamless. Everyone was clear about his own role and so we were freed up to flow with one another.

Rehearsal

To rehearse or not to rehearse? Decide. The bigger or more formal (read: intricate) the event, the stronger it will be with a rehearsal. One rehearsal. I recommend one one-hour meeting involving two quick rehearsals of the ceremony. Everyone in the wedding party should be in attendance. People assigned to deliver a special reading need not attend, but will appreciate a verbal check-in with the officiator just prior to the ceremony.

Begin the rehearsal by introducing the wedding party, the minister or officiator, planner, parents and primary witnesses or attendants (best man/woman). Offer a brief verbal description of how the event will proceed.

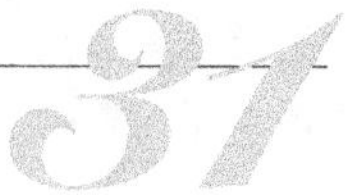

One couple *divided up the responsibilities but did not communicate their expectations to each other. When I asked about a rehearsal, she said, "Oh, Dan is handling that." When I inquired about kids, I heard, "Linda has that covered." When I wanted to know who would give commencement cues to Dan and me, to the flower girls and maid of honor, I was told, "We'll take care of it."*

When I arrived at the wedding site, kids were running everywhere. The bride and groom had not introduced me to the wedding party, so I sought them out. The Best Man did not know if he would hold the rings or not. The groomsmen were clueless about their roles, and the maid of honor told me she would just follow the flower girl, it will be OK (it's not). We stood around for over an hour, in the blazing sun, because no one would start. Finally, I asked the bride if I could signal a start. She was embarrassed but relieved!

Keep it brief (no more than 5 minutes) and simple because people often bring excitement, anxiety and short attention spans to the rehearsal.

Next, position the wedding party in the place *where you want them to be at the completion of the processional*, before the welcoming address would begin. Address each person by their position titles so the participants will associate their role with the position they take, their entry cue, or their part in the ceremony. For example, "Groom stands here . . . bride's mother seated here by usher; maid of honor behind the bride, then bridesmaids one, two . . ."

When it looks as if everyone is in their correct position, have the bride step to the side, or back down the aisle to view the arrangement of attendants, parents, groom, and officiator. Make sure everyone knows where to stand for the ceremony. Then, walk the wedding party out in *reverse order*—bride and groom, flower girl(s) with ring bearer, maid and best man, then pairs of brides' and grooms' attendants. (See Recessional notes)

Now the wedding party is prepared for procession, because now they know where to go.

The first "walk-through" may require a small eternity. There will be questions, some confusion, wrinkled foreheads, chatting, giggling, rude comments, squirming and smiles. The second walk-through should not require anything more than verbal cues, such as, "Okay, now the bridesmaids . . ." Someone usually breaks into a wedding march hum or "da da da-da . . ." Everyone else chimes in and you'll know you're ready!

Do not over-rehearse. With too much attention, children tend to become anxious, and adults become stiff.

Children in the Ceremony

I suggest one person only instruct the children, and everyone in the wedding party needs to know that one set of instructions will go out to the children. That one person must be known by the children, and should be sane, rational and grounded. Nothing is worse for the children than to have several adults telling them what to do, and the person they most rely on for information upset over their clothes or how they walk, or "Oh my God"-ing because the kids get nervous and can't move. Children should be at least 4 to participate, only the most precocious and confident 3 year old should be considered.

Rehearsing children

Let the children watch the adults run through their parts first. This allows the children to see the adults flopping around a bit, taking directions from someone else, and sometimes getting it wrong. Then they can take part knowing that it is okay to not get it perfect. Their part should be very simple, especially for the very young.

Children need one coach, or one sane parent to guide them. A gentle way to guide a three year flower girl, for example: The child's coach stands behind the child and places her (calm) hands on the young one's shoulders. She puts her face near the child's and shows the child where to look. "Do you see that woman in the blue suit, the minister?" I smile. "When she looks at you and nods, you begin your walk; toss some flower petals as you walk. You will walk up there (point) and stand next to Aunt Susan (Maid of Honor)."

The "buddy system" is the best way to rehearse young children. The coach walks with the child, pretending to pluck and toss flower petals. The child imitates the coach. Then, the child does the walk on her own with cues from the coach. If a child bails out at the last minute, let them. Be gracious and thank them for considering playing a part.

Cues for Commencement and Processional

Who will signal the start of the ceremony—Minister, coordinator or planner, bride?

From the guests' point of view, the traditional wedding ceremony is commencing when they see the groom's parents go to their seats. Ushers may have either escorted guests to seats, or someone (planner/coordinator or usher) has quietly asked people to seat themselves. Some ceremonies begin with the minister, groom and groomsmen entering and taking their positions.

Usually, word goes out from the bride to the coordinator that she is ready to begin. The traditional wedding procession begins with her signal: The minister, groom and groomsmen take their positions. The groom's parents are seated. The bride's mother is seated. The music changes for the procession of bride's maids/matrons, maid of honor, ring bearer, and flower bearer. Music may shift again for the bride's entry, on the arm of her escort.

For non-traditional weddings and commitment ceremonies you can decide whether or not to hold to this pattern. Many couples opt to "walk down the aisle" arm in arm. Outdoor ceremonies lend themselves to all sorts of creative arrangements.

The important thing is to decide how the ceremony will begin, and who will signal the start and cue the celebrants. The larger and more formal the event, the more important it is to have one person provide this service.

Recessional

At the conclusion of the traditional ceremony, or after kiss and pronouncement, the newlyweds turn to face their friends and family. I suggest you pause to be announced, or to be applauded and adored. Soak it all in, then walk back to the entrance area at a normal rate of speed.

When bride and groom have recessed beyond the last row of guests, the Flower girl (from the bride's side) and Ring bearer (from the groom's side) approach the center, likewise pause, link arms or hands and walk together. When they are recessed halfway, best man links arms with maid of honor, pause, and then proceed. Attendants from groom and bride continue in this fashion until the wedding party is "off stage". Usually, I remain in place until the wedding party has recessed. I then step up to the front rows and motion to the couple's families to follow the wedding party. The remaining guests follow the parents and family.

Readers/Soloists:

Will the readers stand 'up front' with the celebrants, or rise from their seats for their part?

In standard seating arrangements, I recommend the guest readers be seated at or near the far or lateral end of a row. When they stand to read their part, they need only turn to face the guests to be heard by everyone. It is usually an awkward break in continuity for a guest to leave their seat, walk to the front, and deliver their speech, then return to sit down. If the reader is one of the main witnesses standing with the couple, they need only turn more toward the guests. Keep it simple.

License

Some couples do not want their ceremony and celebration to be interrupted by the license signing. The officiator discretely signs, then the witnesses for sign, and the completed license is passed back to the Best Man, for instance, to handle for the Groom.

I have signed the license before a wedding because we all agreed it would be the best time. And, I have often posted the completed license for the couple, just to make sure it gets mailed and filed before its deadline.

Some couples like to make a small ceremony of the license signing. After the wedding ceremony, or during the Reception, the Bride and Groom, Officiant and witnesses join together over the license for a formal signing and toast. In "domestic partnership" marriages, couples often celebrate the signing with their guests.

In deciding when, consider the flow of the ceremony, and what may happen directly after. You may be whisked away by an anxious photographer, congratulating friends and family, or by each other! Remember, the officiant may want to leave sooner than most of the guests. Personally, I wait for the cake. But it is better to do the signing sooner than later.

In California the standard license has two spaces for witnesses, though only one is required. I suggest you consider special friends, or the groom's parents or grandparents as witness candidates. Witnessing your license can be a sweet little honor for someone you love.

Payment

If you have not yet paid the minister, the license signing is a good time to do so. Please put the payment in an envelope. Thank you.

Asking a friend to officiate

In some states, anyone can apply to officiate a marriage. If you are considering offering the task to a close friend or relative, consider twice. Be very clear about your expectations for their role, and be certain they are able to carry the responsibility you hand to them. Can your candidate "hold a space" for the celebration, lend enough weight to the role to lead a ceremony? Will your friend have sufficient authority and influence with family and other friends? Can he or she lead a rehearsal? Can your friend inspire your community to dedicate itself to the growth and preservation of your marriage? Will your candidate perform your ceremony, your way? Is he/she in affinity with your beliefs and values?

Do you have a backup plan?

Falling Apart

Creating a ceremony requires hundreds of small and large decisions, focused awareness with hundreds of details, choreography of many different elements, personalities, hopes and desires, within a discrete time frame. Throughout the process you may suffer misunderstandings, botched instructions, lost materials and various kinds of people failure. In the midst of chaos, can you hold the thought (trust) that the Universe will protect

your actions and endeavors?

Tibetan Buddhists have a saying worthy of committing to memory: When many little things go wrong, when it appears that things are falling apart—the failures of little things serve to protect the thing that is about to be born, which must be born pure and whole and perfect.

In Addition . . .

Weddings publicize and celebrate your intentions to live in and for love. The ceremony ushers in the beginning of a new level of being together, solidifying the contract that is your relationship. The officiant's duty, therefore, is to hold the space for you to declare those intentions. The officiator adds density to the agreement by witnessing, solemnizing and legitimizing the new contract.

Purpose

You may think you do not need a real minister, just someone to say the words and sign the license. You may be afraid to ask about other services. Or, maybe it hasn't occurred to you that the person you hired to say the magic words is also an adviser or counselor in the realm of the heart and spirit.

Choose an officiant with whom you feel rapport and trust. Your officiant is a neutral third party who represents your spiritual interests within the ceremony, a stand-in for "Who Marries You".

You may also consult your officiant on a variety of matters. Your minister can help you resolve family conflicts and gain perspective on past experiences. You may confide in her regarding any fear or concern you are carrying. She can help you give voice to your hopes and fears, pray and meditate with you, and help you get grounded on your wedding day.

Edification

At the reception, friends and family of the couple always compliment the ceremony (and me, too). They tell me how special the various readings were, or how meaningful the vows, or the rituals. The comment I hear most often? "I loved the way you personalized the ceremony."

I respond by explaining how the couple worked hard on the ceremony, or created the rituals, or wrote their own vows. I add, "Be sure to tell them how much you enjoyed it." In some situations all I can honestly say is that this couple was "involved with the ceremony right from the start, they really made it their own." I love the looks of surprise, renewed

Breathe *Inhale, deeply and slowly. Slowly exhale. Repeat. Repeat. Repeat. Doesn't that feel better? Can you feel yourself relaxing?*

You arrive at the staging area, beautiful and polished, wide open and smiling. You may not remember how you got there. You may not be anywhere near your body. You may still be rushing around in your mind. You have that "deer caught in the headlights" look in your eyes. Breathe. Again. Again.

You have prepared a wonderful, heart-felt statement to read to your beloved. Three words into it, your eyes mist over. You are barely through the first sentence before your voice cracks and the tears flood your eyes. Go ahead, cry. It rarely lasts more than a few seconds. Cry. Breathe. Again. Again. We'll wait. Where would we go?

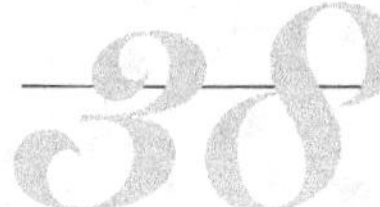

appreciation and awe. And, while the friends and family are telling stories over dinner or cake, I can always find ways to compliment the couple for their character and their devotion, or the chosen event site, the caterers, even the weather.

To edify means to build up. As a minister, I am given much credibility and honor to officiate a ceremony. By edifying the couple, I pass this honor back to them; I build them up to their family and friends. Edification gently reminds guests that this son or daughter, grandson or friend, is now a creative and responsible partner to their lover.

Time

People waiting for the ceremony to start will look at their watches, often not even seeing the time, just exercising the habit of looking. They are not anxious for time to pass; they are excited.

For the few moments of ceremony, time officially stands still. Like children at play, we unbind ourselves. We will not be rushed. No one will call us for dinner. We luxuriate in time stretched, the rules of time bent just for us. No deadlines exist—just life, taking its time.

Part 2

Structure, Content, Flow

My role in the preparation is to help you find your beliefs and values and then represent your spiritual interests within the ceremony. If the words you write, or find, are an apt expression of your beliefs, values and intentions, I need only advise you on the flow, content and structure of the ceremony.

As someone with a little writing and speaking experience, I treat the ceremony you write or compile as I think of the ceremonies I offer you in the next section—as a template or practice piece. I will comb through your practice piece carefully, listening to its tone and rhythms, feeling for its intentions and flow, and watching for needless repeaters and awkward interrupters. Knowing what to prune and pick out of your text may be as important as knowing what to put in.

In this section you will be able to see how a typical ceremony is organized. You will be introduced to all of the various parts with suggestions for their use. Though you may decide not to use some of the parts and/or suggestions for their placement within the ceremony, you will have an understanding of their use with some examples to help you decide.

Chapter 1

Structure

A ceremony, or any ritual for that matter, must have a beginning, a middle and an end. Here are brief descriptions of the structural portions, followed by suggestions for and examples of the pieces that may be contained in each part.

In typical wedding/commitment ceremonies the beginning, or **Commencement**, is comprised of an "Opener" or Welcome, a Statement, an Invocation and often a Prayer. The space held by the officiator is large, open, taking in all the guests. As you will see in the ceremony part descriptions, attendees are spoken to and directed by the officiator. Readings and other rituals placed here are usually for the guest's benefit.

The statements and prayers should support, and lead unerringly, toward the middle, or **Heart** of the ceremony. The Heart expresses intentions through Vows or Promises. The Heart may include special "exchanges" of rings and/or readings, pledges, wine, gifts. The scope of attention and space is narrowed down to the officiator and the couple. Rituals and special readings in the Heart of the ceremony are designed for the couple and usually performed by the couple. This is a very intimate space.

The end part, or **Conclusion**, completes the ceremony with a Blessing and a Pronouncement. It is usually brief. A Blessing or Completion Statement helps to hold the private energetic space for a moment. The Pronouncement certifies the new status of the couple. Then, The Kiss, which seals the promises. The energetic space opens up to the family and friends again. I often introduce the new "Mr. and Mrs." over the din of applause and excitement.

Structure

Processional (assembling)

Commencement

Welcome and Opening Remarks

Statement on Marriage

Invocation

Prayer

Heart

Personal Statements

Vows, Promises, Affirmations

Ring Exchange

Conclusion

Final Statements

Blessing

Pronouncement

Introduction

Recessional (disassembling)

Taking a closer look at:
Commencement

This portion of the ceremony might include the Welcome, Opening Remarks, Statement on Marriage, Invocation and Prayer. Special songs, readings and rituals may be added to open the ceremony, or to assist the transition from one part to another, or to substitute for Invocation or Prayer.

Opening:

Includes opening remarks or welcome statements; can be a simple greeting to focus group attention, or cue the start of the ceremony.

At formal weddings, I offer a greeting before the wedding party proceeds. After the groom's parents and the bride's mother have been seated, I address everyone, "Welcome and Good Afternoon. The Jones and Martin families are honored to have you here to witness and celebrate the joining in marriage of their beloved Janet and Jim."

As the music begins, the wedding party proceeds. "Please stand to receive the Bride," I announce, as she walks toward her groom on the arm of her father or escort. As the bride and her escort stop and the groom takes his place beside her, I may ask the traditional question: "Who gives this woman (or couple) in marriage?" Her parents (or both sets of parents) assent, and the bride takes the arm of her groom. (In rehearsal, I call this the "hand off.")

In a more casual ceremony, I may greet on behalf of the couple, in their presence, just before launching into the Statement. For example, "Good afternoon and welcome, everyone. Joseph and Charlie are delighted to have you here to celebrate their love and commitment on this beautiful day."

How the officiator opens the ceremony depends upon the style and level of formality you think appropriate.

The following examples in quoted italics, are portions of the standard Wedding ceremony from the Church of Natural Grace in San Francisco.

The Statement:

"Marriage is a statement between two people about their affinity and commitment to each other. This ceremony is a time of public declaration about the private understanding and harmony of two souls."

The Statement allows you to share your unique perspective on marriage and commitment. The Statement, a carefully crafted expression of your common values, informs your guests about your beliefs and intentions. It represents the mental level of your contract. By placing the statement at the opening of the ceremony, you help your guests let go of their own expectations for your ceremony, and accept you as mature, discerning partners in relationship.

"They begin the creation of a new life as one: Two separate beings in assistance to each other; each one appointing the other as guardian of his or her freedom and solitude."

The declarative style brings everyone into a more focused and mindful state. The officiator directs the "range" of attention, or energetic space, to be wide open, to include everyone in attendance.

"Sarah Janet Barnes and John Archer Williams have reached a mutual, loving accord which allows them each the space and freedom to create and grow as individuals."

I recommend the officiator use your full names for a somewhat solemn and serious affect, either in the Opening Remarks or Statement. It implies that you and your partner have a contract, an agreement made thoughtfully and carefully. Thereafter, use your first names only. Some couples even use nicknames throughout the remainder of the ceremony.

The Statement may be brief, an attention-getter, a "where-we're-at" statement. You can easily precede or follow this piece with a special reading, ritual or song. Some couples follow the Statement with an open invitation to family and/or friends to make comments, give blessings and best wishes.

The Invocation:

"We are gathered in celebration . . ."

The invocation invites people to gather their energy as a group and as individuals. We can be so busy looking at you, remembering our own wedding, fussing with kids or clothes or cameras, anticipating the next thing . . . we forget to be in the moment. The invocation gives your guests the opportunity to be fully present and alive within their own bodies. Find a creative way to help people to 'arrive.'

"Acknowledge yourself as spirit in your body. Acknowledge each other in this

I think of the Invocation as an invitation into the energetic space within you, as well as the space we create together. Addressing all attendees, I ask you to pause for a moment, breathe and be in your body. I direct your attention inward in order to have your mindful participation. I may ask us all to acknowledge the god of our own heart.

The power of the Invocation rests in uniting being with body, which brings us into present time. When we are fully present we are powerful!

Together, we invoke Spirit.

By giving people time to breathe, reflect and settle in, you give them permission to give back to you from their hearts.

"Now, let us grant Sarah and John total freedom to grow and manifest as individuals within the framework of their mutual love. Allow them to create this marriage in their own way, so that they may best learn from and take delight in one another."

Invocation can be a gentle way of asking people to recognize your capabilities or to step out of your "contract" with each other.

There are many ways to invoke spirit and draw people into accord. Some officiators make a very brief statement followed by a simple ritual. Calling the Four Directions, lighting special incense, "smudging" with white or purple sage, and closing a circle of flower petals around the couple are simple rituals that create a sense of the sacred within the ceremony. See the "***Civil Rites***" section for descriptions and ideas.

The Invocation may be followed by another special reading or blessing. Be sensitive to the mood and tone you are creating. If your words and rituals induce a quiet, sacred space, it may be best to continue in that vein. Make sure your reader or singer can sense the tone, and that the reading or song supports the energetic space.

"On Marriage" by Kahlil Gibran has often been read in place of, or in addition to an Invocation. Versions of the Jewish Seven Blessings, poetry by Rumi or Kabir, or a favorite love song may be inserted to extend the inspirational moment (See Part 3: Words of Love for ideas).

Prayer for the Marriage

Let us Pray—-

"God, let thy blessings now rest upon this man and woman as they enter into this Holy Union."

Together we ask for divine presence, guidance and protection. The Prayer invites God (or "Who marries you") into the marriage contract to ensure a spiritual union. The Prayer elevates the intent of the marriage

contract as it solemnizes the vows and promises you are about to make.

God perspective: Divine Spirit, Creator, Great Spirit, Higher Power . . .

"And as they begin their wedded life today in prayer, so may they continue it—praying for and with each other. Amen"

I sincerely hope this for you, too.

Here is another opportunity to carefully insert something special—after the Prayer and before the Promises. The focus of attention in the Heart of the ceremony will narrow to an intimate space between you and your partner. You may want to insert a meaningful poem or song as a transition piece.

Taking a closer look at:
The Heart

Includes Pledges, Vows and Ring Exchange. May also include personal statements, sharing rituals, gift exchange.

Personal Statements

After Prayers, before Promises—this is the best place for you to read personal statements to each other. You can be boldly sentimental, publicly appreciative, and even humorous. These statements are usually composed in private, they are not compared or shared prior to the ceremony. See examples in Part 3, Special Addresses/Statements.

I draft and insert personal statements into the ceremony text. That way you don't have to carry a sheet of paper, and your statement to your partner becomes a permanent part of the ceremony. What a wonderful way to honor each other—endearing and memorable for everyone! Get out your handkerchiefs.

Promises, Pledges and Vows

"I, Sarah, promise to love you, John, and to live with you this lifetime . . ."

Vows are your personal promises to live with your partner for life, for love. They may be phrased as a question to which you answer, "I do" or "I will," or they may be promise statements, called Pledges, that you make to each other. Or both. The vows are usually in question format so you will make your promise to Spirit and your partner, through the Officiant.

The Promises should not be upstaged by additional readings, which may interrupt the quiet and private space. Hold and savor the moment.

Sharing Rituals

"By sharing this Wine Glass, Two become One"

An optional sharing of wine or water, flowers or gifts with a short statement helps bring the vows to completion. Candle lighting, bell or bowl ringing, releasing butterflies or birds—these are additional ways to bring uniqueness to the Heart of the ceremony.

Keep it Simple: Ritual objects should be readily available, held by an attendant or resting on a table nearby.

Ring Exchange

". . . an outward visible Sign of an inward Spiritual Unity . . ."

Seal the vows with a ring exchange.

Attendants can hold the rings until they are needed. If the rings are tied to the ring bearer's pillow, make sure they can easily be removed.

Usually, I take the rings from the pillow, or the attendant, and bless them. Then I offer the rings to the couple for the exchange. Some couples opt to read statements as they place a ring on their partner's finger. Have these short statements included in the officiator's copy of the text—don't torture yourself trying to memorize a special statement, or worry about carrying a small piece of paper.

Taking a closer look at:
The Conclusion

May include Blessings, a Pronouncement, The Kiss, Introduction . . . .

Blessing

"May you find what you seek as you walk your path . . ."

Again, keep it simple and brief. Let the highpoints be your personal statements, vows and ring exchanges. Let the Blessings be the "God-seal" on your marriage.

For the Blessing, I would have you join hands; I place my hand over yours and we pray together. The energetic space is small, the blessing is private. Amen. The Blessing often takes the place of a pronouncement. But you may certainly have both.

In religious church services there are often additional statements and

prayers after the vows and ring exchange. Personally, I think people stop listening after "I do." After you kiss, there's no holding folks in their chairs. End it.

Pronouncement and Kiss

You may be pronounced as husband and wife or New Family, or Life Partners. Decide the pronouncement with your Officiator based upon how you see your new partnership.

"Will you honor each other with a kiss?"

And you will.

And that ends the ceremony! Now, turn toward your family and friends. You may wish to be introduced or announced, "Congratulations, Newlyweds!" or "Family and Friends, Maria and Joan!" or "Mr. and Mrs. John Warren" or "John and Sarah Warren" . . .

Your friends and family will be applauding and crying and making all sorts of noises, so it may not matter if you are announced or not. Sometimes, I just say, "Let's congratulate Maria and Joan!" and I begin the applause.

Take a moment to soak up all that adoration. Then, the Recessional. And, party time!

Chapter 2

Content and Flow

Content is what you put into your ceremony

Input

What qualities of *heart, mind* and *spirit* really matter to you? Whether you write your own, or compile from existing writings, each piece of writing needs to be in alignment with your values.

Heart values are words and concepts you can feel in your body. They have a rightness about them, which bypasses logic but not sense. What are your Heart values? Kindness, Compassion, Devotion, Trust, Loyalty, Truth, Courage, Love . . . ?

Mind values help you make sense, give you as sense of order or a container for feelings; they make the emotional rational. What are your Mind values? Family, Friendship, Understanding, Common Goals and Values, Intimacy, Appreciation . . . ?

Spirit values are words that uplift and inspire. These values raise our awareness to the highest and best possibilities. What are your Spirit values? Inspiration, Mystery, Gratitude, Purpose, Faith, Light, Hope . . . ?

Values lie beneath words *"The Art of Marriage" (attributed to Wilferd Arlan Peterson) is a piece that appeals to many couples. It is often used as an opening statement to a wedding ceremony. Notice the values and beliefs being expressed in each statement.*

The Art of Marriage

A good marriage must be created. (value: personal responsibility)

In a marriage the little things are the big things.

It is never being too old to hold hands. (value: affection)

It is remembering to say "I love you" at least once a day.

It is never going to sleep angry. (value: resolution)

It is having a mutual sense of values and common objectives.

It is standing together facing the world. (value: unity, support)

It is forming a circle of love that gathers in the whole family. (value: relationships)

It is speaking words of appreciation and demonstrating gratitude in thoughtful ways.
(value: kindness, appreciation...)

It is having the capacity to forgive and forget. (value: faith, trust)

It is giving each other an atmosphere in which each can grow.

It is a common search for the good and the beautiful.

It is not only marrying the right person, it is being the right partner
(value: character...)

The Statements, Pledges, Rituals and Blessings in your ceremony should contain thoughts that adequately express these values. Looking over what you write or compile,

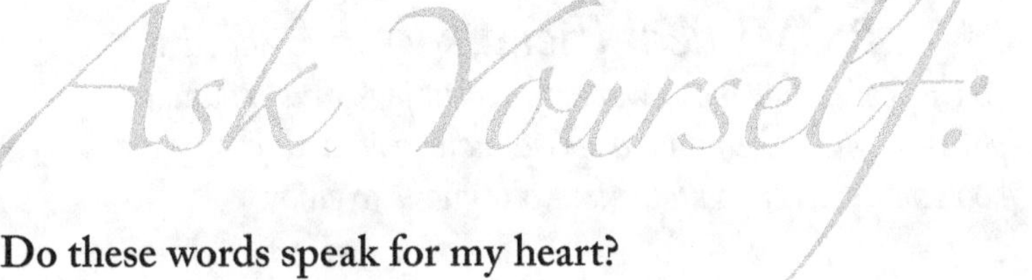

Do these words speak for my heart?

Do they make sense to my personality?

Do they inspire me to live and love to the best of my ability?

P.S. My dear friend, Rev. Rose Taylor advises you to collect all those wonderful prunings and redundant phrases. Scribe them into a special notebook, and display the book on the reception table for your guests to enjoy.

Output

Advice from professional writers is well taken when creating your own ceremony or borrowing another's words. Write it all, everything you want to say—the lovely phrases, hopefulness and wishes. All the compliments and promises and every well-said thought that expresses how you hope you will be as a life partner. All of it.

Then, put on your gloves and start weeding. Omit anything that doesn't make sense, except to you. Eliminate repetitive phrases and ideas, themes or concepts. There will be many of these. Similar ideas will dress themselves differently within different parts of the ceremony. They will be abundant in your writing. You are redundant for the same reasons I am in writing to you—because you are practicing saying it well so you can get it right. From your desire to get it right, you may feel pressured to say more in your ceremony precisely because it is your ceremony—and one of the most important events of your life.

"Look for the clutter in your writing and prune it ruthlessly. Be grateful for everything you can throw away. Re-examine each sentence you put on paper. Is every word doing new work? Can any thought be expressed with more economy? Is anything pompous or pretentious or faddish? Are you hanging on to something useless just because you think it's beautiful?

Simplify, simplify."

William Zinsser, *On Writing Well*

Here are a few questions that may help you 'red flag' the areas of content that need help.

• Do these words adequately express our spiritual beliefs and personal values?

• Does this make sense? Would the average person understand it?

• Can it be said more simply (simple=eloquent)?

• Does this 'speak' well? (someone has to *say* these words to your family and friends)

• Does this piece fit well? This question helps me gauge the word-fit within the individual piece, the piece-fit within the larger part, and the parts with respect to the overall flow.

Finally, **read** your work aloud. Read your piece at a pace slightly slower than normal rate of speech. If you have more than 8 minutes of minister monologue, go back to weeding. Or, look to see where you can appropriately interject a song, poem or special reading by someone other than the officiant. Focus fades quickly. The attention should be on you and the thoughts and feelings being conveyed by the piece, not on the messenger.

Flow is what happens when what you put together works together

Not only should each sentence flow into the next, and each paragraph make way for the next, but also each part of the ceremony should easily lead to the next part. Each part expresses a key thought or idea—a *pearl*. Notice if the pearls of thought string together, each piece leading to the next piece. Do they build on one another? Support one another? Do the minister's words or parts work well with the additional readings or rituals? Think it, read it, envision the ceremony as a whole, a collection of parts, or, a string of pearls.

Special readings, songs, and some rituals can be complimentary additions to the flow, or they can be jarring intruders. I recommend placing songs, poems and readings in the **Commencement** part of the ceremony. I believe the Heart of the Ceremony—the couple's vows, ring exchange, and personal statements—should stand alone, uninterrupted by additional readings. Remember, in the **Heart**, the energetic space is intimate. It is usually awkward to re-open this private space to guest readers.

I also feel strongly about keeping the space closed through the **Conclusion**. Let the Heart create its own quiet momentum, and bring the ceremony to a simple and swift conclusion. Don't allow anticlimactic additions to steal from the Heart.

Now you're ready to find the magic words!

In Part III you will find samples of complete ceremonies, followed by sample parts of ceremonies. In addition, I've included various rituals and blessings, poems and prose to consider for your ceremony. Enjoy and best of luck.

Footnote:
**I draft and insert all special readings into the ceremony booklet I prepare for each couple. I make copies of those readings on matching paper for each presenter as well. It makes a complete and attractive presentation, and a keepsake. Ask your Officiator for the "working copy" of your ceremony.*

Part 3

Supplemental Section

1 The Long and Short of it:

A Ceremony Sampler

In this chapter I have arranged a few whole ceremonies. The time notations are approximate and do not include any additional material nor the processional or recessional. Even a five-minute spoken ceremony can grow into a twenty to forty minute event with the addition of musical interludes, slow processions and rituals.

Ceremony 1

(About 15 minutes) Here is a typical ***Church of Natural Grace*** wedding ceremony. Many couples use this ceremony as a template—they change the text, add or delete words, or substitute with other readings to make it their own.

Opening Remarks/Welcome

Statement on Marriage

Marriage is a statement between two people about their affinity and commitment to each other. This ceremony is a time of public declaration about the private understanding and harmony of two souls.

Marriage is a bond of trust, in which each partner allows the other the most intimate and open expression of his or her self, in a spirit of love, faith and truth. It is open communication between two beings for support and sharing of experience and information.

They begin the creation of a new life as one: Two separate beings in assistance to each other; each one appointing the other as guardian of his or her freedom and solitude.

Clark Kent and Lois Lane have reached a mutual loving accord which allows them each the space and freedom to create and grow as individuals.

Invocation

We are gathered in celebration, to share in the overflowing joy manifested by Lois and Clark's love for one another. Let us take a moment to gather and purify our energy, so that this occasion may be one of great peace and delight for us all.

Close your eyes with us if you like, take a few slow, deep breaths. Allow yourself to call back all your energy into yourself here today, so you can experience this moment as fully as possible. Acknowledge yourself as spirit in your body. Acknowledge each other in this place as spirit also, each of you with your own life and path.

Now, let us grant Clark and Lois total freedom to grow and manifest as individuals within the framework of their mutual love. Allow them the space to create this marriage in their own way, so that they may best learn from, and take delight in, one another.

Lois and Clark, as you begin this partnership, receive from us the greatest gifts we can give: Freedom to be and space to create your own reality.

Prayer for the Marriage

God, let thy Blessings now rest upon this man and woman
as they enter into this Holy Union.

Let all the days before them be bright and happy.

If pain or sorrow enters their life, help them to bear it together—
with compassion be joined all the more closely by it.

Let them be aware of each other's space.

Grant that their house, wherever it shall be, may be for them the happiest
place. Grant that their home, the body, be nurtured with mutual love,
honor, and respect.

Let their spirits dwell within. Let their time together be one of growth,
ever learning from one another.

And as they begin their wedded life today in prayer, so may they continue
it—

Praying for and with each other.

Amen.

Promises

Do you, Clark, promise to love Lois, and to live with her through this
lifetime; to build with her a new home that is a place of love, joy, sharing
and growing?

"I do."

Do you, Clark, promise to be with her in all of her triumphs and
adversities, and in her happiness, to give her your best counsel, and above
all, freedom to be Lois?

"I do."

Do you, Lois, promise to love Clark, and to live with him through this
lifetime; to build with him a new home that is a place of love, joy, sharing
and growing?

"I do."

Do you, Lois, promise to be with him in all of her triumphs and
adversities, and in his happiness, to give him your best counsel, and above
all, freedom to be Clark?

"I do."

Wine Sharing

Wine is the symbol of Life
The flow within our bodies
By sharing this Wine Glass, two become one
A part of the Whole, each separate,
Yet united in Love.

Ring Exchange

The Ring symbolizes the continuous
Circle of Eternal Life
The ring is a reminder of the love
between Lois and Clark.
It is an outward visible Sign
of an inward Spiritual Unity.

Blessing

May the Blessings of the Divine Spirit be with you.
May you walk in the Light.
May you reflect the Power and Love of the Light.
May you find what you seek as you walk your path with one another.

Will you honor each other with a kiss?
Congratulations, Clark and Lois Kent!

Recessional

If I talk slowly, the preceding ceremony could stretch to 20 minutes!
It is usually about 12-15 minutes in length, unless the couple adds special
readings, songs or other rituals.

Ceremony 2

Short and Sweet: The following is a five-minute ceremony performed for a couple that wanted very little fuss, no pomp nor circumstance. We assembled in their hotel suite with a witness and one bottle of champagne. After the ceremony and a brief toast, this couple attended a small dinner party in the adjoining room, held in their honor. Sweet.

Welcome

Opening

Within the circle of its love, marriage encompasses all of life's most important relationships. A wife and a husband are each other's best friend, confidant, lover, teacher, listener, and critic. There may come times when one partner is heartbroken or ailing, and the love of the other may resemble the tender caring of a parent for a child.

When two people pledge to love and care for each other in marriage, they create a spirit unique to themselves, which binds them closer than any spoken or written words. Marriage is a promise, a potential, made in the hearts of two people who love, which takes a lifetime to fulfill.

It is with this understanding then, that you, Sally, and you Harry, have come to form a covenant between you in the presence of family and friends who rejoice with you in the making of this important commitment.

Promises

Harry: I promise to love you, Sally, and to live with you through this lifetime; to build with you a new home that is a place of love, joy, sharing and growing.

I promise to be with you in all of your triumphs and adversities, and in your happiness, to give you my best counsel, and above all, freedom to be yourself.

Sally: I promise to love you, Harry, and to live with you through this lifetime; to build with you a new home that is a place of love, joy, sharing and growing.

I promise to be with you in all of your triumphs and adversities, and in your happiness, to give you my best counsel, and above all, freedom to be yourself.

Harry: With this ring I thee wed.

Sally: With this ring I thee wed.

May Harry and Sally keep this covenant; may the inspiration of this hour remain with them. May they, trusting each other, trust life and may they continue to love each other forever. May the love, companionship and friendliness of the home be an inspiration to family and loved ones.

No pronouncement, just a kiss and a presentation!

Ceremony 3

(5-10 minutes)

Pilar and Bob each spent an hour with the Compendium of this book. Together, they compared their selections and found that most were similar and some the same. They negotiated small parts from three ceremonies, re-arranged them and changed the focus (pronouns) of the closing statement. The following ceremony took place in the late afternoon of an astonishingly clear winter day, on the rooftop of a historic San Francisco hotel, witnessed by four of their closest friends.

Welcome

Opening Statement

We are gathered in celebration, to share in the overflowing joy manifested by Bob and Pilar's love for one another.

Within the circle of its love, marriage encompasses all of life's most important relationships. A wife and a husband are each other's best friend, confidant, lover, teacher, listener, and critic. There may come times when one partner is heartbroken or ailing, and the love of the other may resemble the tender caring of a parent for a child.

When two people pledge to love and care for each other in marriage, they create a spirit unique to themselves, which binds them closer than any spoken or written words. Marriage is a promise, a potential, made in the hearts of two people who love, which takes a lifetime to fulfill.

It is with this understanding then, that you, Bob, and you Pilar, have come to form a covenant between you in the presence of friends who rejoice with you in the making of this important commitment.

I remind all of you that you have been invited here for a holy purpose, not just to witness, but to participate fully with your thoughts and prayers, asking God to bless this couple and their married life. You are here because this couple feels close to you and asks that you join with them in this dedication of sacred purpose. You represent symbolically all the people in the world who will be touched in any way by the life of this couple. By your presence here you accept responsibility for helping Pilar and Bob and encouraging them in the new relationship into which they are about to enter.

Would anyone like to offer a comment, a blessing or wish for Pilar and Bob?

(Comments of four friends added about 7 minutes to this 5-minute ceremony)

Promises

Do you, Bob, promise to love Pilar with an open and honest heart? Do you promise to cherish, comfort and support Pilar and willingly choose to live your life with her both freed and joined by love?

"I Do"

Do you Pilar, accept these solemn vows to be the foundation of your new life together?

"I Do"

Do you, Pilar, promise to love Bob with an open and honest heart? Do you promise to cherish, comfort and support Bob and willingly choose to live your life with him both freed and joined by love?

"I Do"

Do you Bob, accept these solemn vows to be the foundation of your new life together?

"I Do"

Ring Exchange

The Ring symbolizes the continuous Circle of Eternal Life. This ring is a reminder of the love between Bob and Pilar. It is an outward visible sign of an inward spiritual unity.

Bob and Pilar, may you keep this covenant; may the inspiration of this hour remain with you. May you, trusting each other, trust life and may you continue to love each other forever. May the love, companionship, and friendliness of your home be an inspiration to family and loved ones.

Will you honor each other with a kiss?

Now I have the pleasure of presenting Mr. and Mrs. Hope

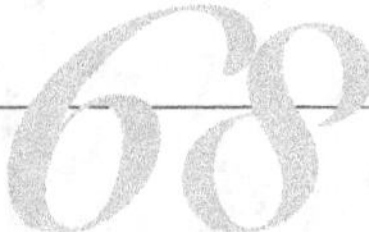

2 Ceremony Dim Sum

A Compendium of Parts

Like an auto dismantler, I have "parted out" ceremonies into their constituent pieces. Most pieces have come to me from couples working on their own ceremonies. I do not know their precise origins, and most have been adjusted to reflect a particular perspective. Care has been taken to trace the ownership and obtain permission, if necessary, for text provided by authors other than myself.

As if selecting from a Dim Sum of wonderful treats, you may mix and match pieces that are yummy in the mind's eye and pleasing to the heart's palate.

Opening Statements

Statement 1: "The Art of Marriage" attributed to Wilferd Arlan Peterson

A good marriage must be created

In a marriage the little things are the big things.

It is never being too old to hold hands.

It is remembering to say "I love you" at least once a day.

It is never going to sleep angry.

It is having a mutual sense of values and common objectives.

It is standing together facing the world.

I is forming a circle of love that gathers in the whole family.

It is speaking words of appreciation and demonstrating gratitude in thoughtful ways.

It is having the capacity to forgive and forget.

It is giving each other an atmosphere in which each can grow.

It is not only marrying the right person,

It is being the right partner.

The Art of Marriage

Statement 2: Reflections on Marriage

from "Weddings from the Heart" by Daphne Rose Kingma

Marriage is the joining of two lives, the mystical, physical, and emotional union of two human beings who have separate families and histories, separate tragedies and destinies. Two individuals, each of whom has a unique and life-shaping past, willingly choose to set aside the solitary exploration of themselves to discover who they are in the presence of one another.

In a sense the person we marry is a stranger about whom we have a magnificent hunch. The person we choose to marry is someone we love, but his depths, her intimate intricacies, we will come to know only in the long unraveling of time. We know enough about our beloved to know that we love him, to imagine that, as time goes on, we will come to enjoy her even more, become even more of ourselves in her presence. To our knowledge we add our willingness to embark on the journey of getting to know him, of coming to see her, ever so wonderfully more.

Marriage is also the incubator of love, the protected environment in which a love that is personal and touching and real can grow and, as a consequence of that growth, develop in us our highest capabilities as loving human beings. We marry not only to be loved, to have a place and a person to whom we can come home, to have our own needs met; we marry also to come into the presence of our own capacity to love: to nurture, to heal, to give, and to forgive.

For love received is needs met; but love delivered is compassion. Loving one another is the beginning of compassion. And it is in the practice of this radiant love that true marriage calls forth the best in us, the most we can ever become.

Statement 3: Statement on Marriage from the Church of Natural Grace

Marriage is a statement between two people about their affinity and commitment to each other. This ceremony is a time of public declaration about the private understanding and harmony of two souls.

Marriage is a bond of trust, in which each partner allows the other the most intimate and open expression of his or her self, in a spirit of love, faith and truth. It is open communication between two beings for support and sharing of experience and information.

They begin the creation of a new life as one: Two separate beings in assistance to each other; each one appointing the other as guardian of his or her freedom and solitude.

Clark Kent and Lois Lane have reached a mutual loving accord which allows them each the space and freedom to create and grow as individuals. Let us help them develop the wisdom, patience, and courage to create this marriage in their own way, so that they may best learn from and take delight in one another. Clark and Lois, as you begin this partnership, receive from us the greatest gifts we can give: our love, respect, and support to help you create your own fulfilling marriage.

Statement 4:

Clark and Lois, two people who were once strangers to each other, come here to join each other as husband and wife, as lovers, as companions and

as friends.

Marriage unites two souls through a joyous bond of love, mutual respect, and commitment.

Marriage is a journey where two travelers share a common path, sharing their burdens and choosing a course together.

Marriage is a flame that is reignited every day.

Marriage is an arena where fear, shyness and embarrassment yield to courage, intimacy and humor.

Marriage is the pen and paper used to express our deepest longings, and heart-felt passions.

Most of all, marriage is a partnership where each partner shares responsibility and authority. Together, the partners thoughtfully consider the values, opinions, needs, and desires of the other. When they are blessed with success and happiness, they share in the joy and celebration of that success. When they encounter hardship or failure, they draw from one another comfort, strength, and the resolve to try again. Through the partnership of marriage, two are able to live life more fully together than they could alone.

Clark Kent and Lois Lane welcome you, honored guests, to witness their marriage.

Statement 5:

Within the circle of its love, marriage encompasses all of life's most important relationships. A wife and a husband are each other's best friend, confidant, lover, teacher, listener, and critic. There may come times when one partner is heartbroken or ailing, and the love of the other may resemble the tender caring of a parent for a child.

When two people pledge to love and care for each other in marriage, they create a spirit unique to themselves, which binds them closer than any spoken or written words. Marriage is a promise, a potential, made in the hearts of two people who love, which takes a lifetime to fulfill.

It is with this understanding, then that you, Bob, and you, Julia, have come to form a covenant between you in the presence of family and friends who rejoice with you in the making of this important commitment.

Statement 6:

Today you, Gertrude, and you, Alice, are surrounded by family and friends. I know that I reflect the feelings of everyone here when I say that we wish you a full, long and happy life together, and that your personal and shared dreams become fulfilled.

You have come today to let this relationship build a spiritual pathway with respect, love and joy. In this lifetime you have chosen to share the journey, side by side, illuminating one another's path, supporting one another's journey. When we give what is most vibrant and enduring in us, we make the world suddenly come alive for another. To be vulnerable, to enter into the experience of another requires uncommon integrity, courage and gentleness. Love is one of the most profound experiences offered to humanity. At its best, it deepens our personalities and makes life more meaningful. Such love can call forth the best qualities in each of you. Therefore, marriage is not to be entered into lightly, but with certainty and mutual respect. You come together, each with a treasure of qualities and talents, and as you share and respect one another, always more fully, your lives will grow and blossom.

In your day to day companionship, enjoy the time spent together, and share the experiences of times spent apart. A good partnership can be recreated each day, out of everyday acts. Be tender to each other, and be forgiving, treasuring the time you share. And be truthful, so that you can always trust. A marriage that lasts is one in which each person feels the freedom to be who they are, to be true to themselves, while growing in support and understanding of the other. So choose to marry because you belong with each other, not to each other.

Invocations

Invocation 1:

We are gathered in celebration, to share in the overflowing joy manifested by Lois' and Clark's love for one another.

I remind all of our guests that you have been invited here for a holy purpose, not just to witness, but to participate fully with your thoughts and prayers, asking God to bless this couple and their married life. You are here because this couple feels close to you and asks that you join with them in this dedication of sacred purpose. You represent symbolically all the people in the world who will be touched in any way by the life of this couple. By your presence here you accept responsibility for helping Clark and Lois and encouraging them in the new relationship into which they are about to enter.

To this end, I invite you to close your eyes, take a deep breath and bring yourselves into this present moment, so that this occasion may be one of great peace and delight for us all. *(pause)*

Now, let us grant Clark and Lois total freedom to grow and manifest as individuals within the framework of their mutual love. Allow them the space to create this marriage in their own way, so that they may best learn from and take delight in one another.

Invocation 2:

Lois and Clark you stand at the center of the circle
where all things meet their opposites:

Male and Female

Darkness and Light

Spirit and Matter

That which makes each whole and complete
just as you two are about to join as one.

Invocation 3:

Dearly Beloved, we have come together, family and friends, in the presence of God, to uphold Lois and Clark as they make their vows of Marriage.

We celebrate with them the love they have discovered in each other, and we support their decision to commit themselves to one another for the rest of their lives. It is a relationship entered into thoughtfully, reverently, with gratitude for the past and hope for the future.

Invocation 4:

Beloved,

Let us love one another

Because love is of God;

Everyone who loves is begotten of God

And has knowledge of God.

The man without love has known nothing of God,

For God is love.

Love, then, consists in this:

Not that we have loved God,

But that he has loved us.

If God has loved us so,

We must have the same love for one another.

No one has ever seen God.

Yet if we love one another

God dwells in us,

And his love is brought to perfection in us.

We have come to know and to believe in the love God has for us.

God is love,

And he who abides in love

Abides in God, and God in him

1 John 4:17–12; 16; 18–19

Invocation 5:

*This is one version of the **Jewish Seven Blessings***

Blessed are You, God, who brings forth fruit from the vine.

Blessed are You, God, who shapes the universe.

Blessed are You, Holy One of blessing, who fashions each person.

We bless You, God for forming each person in your image.

You have planted within us a vision of You and given us the means that we may flourish through time.

Blessed are You, Creator of humanity.

Rejoice and be glad you who have wandered homeless. In joy have you gathered with your sisters and brothers. Blessed is the joy of our gathering.

Let these loving friends taste the bliss You gave to the first man and woman in the garden of Eden.

Blessed are You, the Presence who dwells with bride and groom in delight.

Blessed are You, God, Source of the universe, who lights the world with happiness and contentment, love and companionship, peace and friendship, bridegroom and bride.

May we all see the day when the sounds of joy fill the streets of the world—the voice of the groom and the voice of the bride, the happy shouts of their friends and companions. We bless You, God, who brings bride and groom together to rejoice in each other.

Invocation 6:

Here is a simple introduction to a special reading which substitutes for an Invocation:

We are gathered in celebration so that you, their closest friends (friends and family), may witness and share in Lois and Clark's love for one another. Jimmy Olson will read the Invocation chosen personally by Lois and Clark, as it serves best to define their marriage.

This passage is from "The Prophet" by Kahlil Gibran . . .

Invocation 7:

We are gathered to celebrate the joining of Clark Kent and Jimmy Olson in marriage. Clark and Jimmy have been thinking, planning, and preparing for this occasion for many months. As witnesses to this ceremony, let us take time to consider what this occasion means to us.

Close your eyes, take a deep breath, and think of someone for whom you care deeply. Recall some unique quality about that person that made you love them—anything unique to them. Feel yourself enter into the space of love. *pause*

Now open your eyes and, with this feeling of love, let us create a symbolic space in which Clark and Jimmy may join together. The wedding canopy, the *huppah*, is open on all sides to signify that visitors will always be welcome in their home—though it is a space that they will inhabit alone.

As they begin their new partnership, let us allow Clark and Jimmy to learn from and take delight in the company of one another. And let them receive from us the greatest gifts we can give—our love and support.

Special Addresses/Statements

Special Address/Statement 1:

Mom and Dad, I want to thank you for enabling me, with your love and light, to reach this place of serious commitment. 'Marriage is compromise,' you always said, 'but never hard work.' It is because of your example of a marriage full of laughter, graceful compromise, and above all, untiring love, that I am able to embrace Brian with my full heart.

From drama practice, to swim team, to piano recitals, neither of you ever missed a meet, a play, or a performance. You sat through three productions of 'You're a Good Man Charlie Brown' (and 20 other plays) not to mention the dress rehearsals, and you knew every line, every song by heart. I had the most extravagant birthday parties I can ever hope to have. There was always a welcome brigade at the airport every time I came home from a trip. You are, and always have been my greatest advocates. You praised my achievements, no matter how small. You have given me love and support when I needed it most and deserved it least. Your love for me has been the foundation for all the love I have available to give.

Today, it is more than Brian and my blood that is joined; it is ours as well. With this marriage, God joins our two families. With this in mind, I ask you to take Brian as your son. I ask all of my family to take him into your hearts, for he is beloved to me.

Special Address/Statement 2:

Mom and Dad. I want to thank you for raising me with love and compassion. You taught me the meaning of commitment and how to be a caring person. You enabled me to forge into this life long relationship with Jennifer.

You went to every sporting event. "Stop being a spectator" still rings in my ears. You played countless holes of golf with me. You were cub scout leaders and you worked the snack bar at my basketball games. You moved our family to Arizona because of my asthma. From taking care of me when I was very sick as a young boy to filling out my college applications, you always supported me and wanted the best for me.

My sister, Kelli, thank you for putting up with me and letting me make fun of you for so many years. I promise to never stop. Thanks for being one of my best friends. I cherish growing up with you.

Now, I am opening up our wonderful family. I ask that you take this woman, Jennifer, into your hearts, that she might live from this day as your daughter and sister, for she is dear and beloved to me.

Special Address/Statement 3:
Hayyim Schneid, Marriage

In Hebrew both the word for man, Eesh, and that for a woman, Esha, are composed of three letters, two of which are identical: ESH—meaning fire. The additional letters represent God's name. Thus, the Talmud explains, when a man and woman live together harmoniously they add the presence of the Almighty to their marriage; however, if their marriage is unhappy the only common factor is the presence of a consuming fire.

Special Address/Statement 4:
Things we can learn from a dog.

Never pass up the opportunity to go for a joyride.

When loved ones come home, always run to greet them.

When it's in your best interest, practice obedience.

Let others know when they've invaded your territory.

Take naps and stretch before rising.

Run, romp and play daily.

Eat with gusto and enthusiasm. Stop when you've had enough.

Be loyal.

Never pretend to be something you're not.

If what you want lies buried, dig until you find it.

When someone is having a bad day, be silent, sit close by and nuzzle them gently.

Thrive on attention and let people touch you.

Avoid biting when a simple growl will do.

On warm days, stop to lie on your back in the grass.

On hot days, drink lots of water and lay under a shady tree.

When you're happy, dance around and wag your entire body.

No matter how often you're scolded, don't buy into the guilt thing and pout . . . run right back and make friends.

Delight in the simple joy of a long walk.

Prayers

Prayer 1: Prayer for the Marriage Service

To both of you, I enjoin you to release at this time all impediments to your joy. In this moment may you forgive each other any past transgressions, that you might enter this marriage reborn. You are given the chance to begin your lives again this day. Receive God's gifts on this day, as He receives so fully the gift of your love for each other.

Let us pray—

God, let thy Blessings now rest upon this man and woman as they enter into this Holy Union.

Let all the days before them be bright and happy.

If pain or sorrow enters their life, help them to bear it together – with compassion be joined all the more closely by it.

Let them be aware of each other's space. Grant that their house, wherever it shall be, may be for them the happiest place. Grant that their home, the body, be nurtured with mutual love, honor and respect. Let their spirits dwell within. Let their time together be one of growth, ever-learning from one another.

And as they begin their wedded life today in prayer, so may they continue it – praying for and with each other

AMEN.

Prayer 2:

Divine Spirit, let thy blessings rest upon these partners as they enter into this holy union.

Clark and Jimmy, may you grow in the light of each other's love.

If there be any competition between you, let it be who can be the first to initiate an act of love; the first to give and to forgive; the first to reach out and touch; the first to give comfort and support; the first to praise and encourage. For as long as love is allowed to flow between you, your lives and your marriage will be vibrant and thriving.

May you reach for each other, not to fill your emptiness, but to discover your fullness.

May you need one another, but not out of lack.

May you want one another, but not out of weakness.

May you entice one another, but never compel.

May you embrace one another, but never possess.

May you have love and find it in loving each other.
AMEN

Prayer 3: Serenity Prayer

(Attributed to Reinhold Niebuhr who attributes it to Friedrich Oetinger, an 18th century theologian)

God grant me the serenity to accept the things I cannot change

Courage to change the things I can

And the wisdom to know the difference.

Amen

Prayer 4: Lord's Prayer

Our Father, who art in heaven

Hallowed be Thy name.

Thy kingdom come; Thy will be done

On Earth as it is in Heaven.

Give us this day our daily bread

And forgive us our trespasses as we forgive those who trespass against us.

Lead us not into temptation but deliver us from evil.

For Thine is the kingdom and the power forever

Amen

Prayer 5:

We ask a blessing on this man and woman as they enter into this holy union.

To this moment they bring the dreams of their souls and the fullness of their hearts. Let all the days before them be bright and happy.

Grant that in the moments of life's pain and bitter fruit they be given the remembrance of their joy on this day, to be a balm for their pain. Let them remember that the sweetness of life's joys and delights can only be felt in contrast to the bitterness of tears and sorrow.

Grant them wisdom when they face adversity, faith when there is doubt, laughter when there is discord, and love in every moment. Bring to these companions mirth, joy, harmony, peace and gladness.

Prayer 6: The Aramaic Lord's Prayer

Translated by Ken Rothman, 1997

O Source of All That Is, Name of Names,

Breath of All Unfolding.

Pour out Your Divine Influence and express Your whirling radiance through the boundaries of the universe.

Wed Limitless Substance with form—make Divine Potential manifest.

Extend the creative power of Your Primal Will and bind to it all living things.

From this space, we grow daily in our understanding and application of the One Law, which generates all things.

And our unblemished connection with you is renewed, just as we see the Christ in others.

Let us not be blown about by surface appearances:

Rather free us from barriers to deeper knowing.

For you are the fertile field, the Life Force and the Seed, unfolding in perfect harmony through endless cycles of manifestation.

Truly, from this ground all actions spring.

Vows, Pledges & Promises

Many couples choose to make a declarative statement or pledge to their partner. They make their statement in turn or together, then the Officiant confirms their pledge with an Affirmation in question form.

Vow, Pledge or Promise 1:

Clark (Lois/Jimmy),

I give to you my promise that from this day forward, you shall not walk alone,

May we walk together through all things.

I promise to love you,

to build with you a new home that is a place of love, joy, sharing, and growing,

to be with you in all of your triumphs and adversities, happiness and sorrow

to laugh with you in joy,

to give you my best counsel,

to do my best - I shall always try

and above all, I promise to love you for who you are.

I feel so blessed and honored to call you my husband (wife/partner).

Vow, Pledge or Promise 2:

I promise to love you

To remain honest and faithful to you,

To be available for you when you are in pain or grief

And when you are filled with happiness

I promise to challenge you always,

To support and nurture you

And to be receptive to the gift of your love

I love you with all my heart,

And I will love you for the rest of my life.

Vow, Pledge or Promise 3:

I, Clark, declare that I love you, Jimmy: your generosity, your loyalty and tenderness. I promise to give you support, friendship and peace with gentle care and unwavering trust.

The Officiant affirms the commitment by asking each individual in turn, or both together: **(V4)**

Vow, Pledge or Promise 4:

Officiant: Do you Clark, accept these solemn vows to be the foundation of your new life together?

"I Do"

Vow, Pledge or Promise 5: another version of declaration and affirmation

Lois, I promise to love and cherish you in this life and build with you a new home that is a place of love, joy and sharing. I promise to be with you in all your triumphs and adversities, your laughter and sorrows. I promise to give you my best council, and above all freedom to be who you are.

Lois declares to Clark

Officiant: Do you Clark, accept these solemn vows to be the foundation of your new life together?

"I Do"

Vow, Pledge or Promise 6:

Do you, Lois, promise to love and to live with Clark through this lifetime and to build with him a new home that is a place of love? *I Do*

Do you, Lois, promise to honor Clark with your body, uphold him with your strength and nourish him with your affection? *I Do*

Do you, Lois, promise to be with Clark in all of his triumphs and happiness as well as through all of his adversities? *I Do*

And do you, Lois, promise to be the guardian of Clark's spirit, to help him be steadfastly in the presence of himself, and to nurture that self to full flower? *Yup*

Vow, Pledge or Promise 7:

I, Tom, promise to love you, Sylvia, to listen to you, laugh with you , and share my life with you.

Officiant: Do you, Tom, take Sylvia to be your lawfully wedded wife, to live with her in sickness and in health, for better or for poorer, and to love and respect her as long as you both shall live?

"I Do"

Vow, Pledge or Promise 8:

Do you, Jimmy (and Clark), take Clark (each other) to be your (lawfully wedded wife/husband) life partner, to create a life with him (each other) in good times and bad, in wealth and poorness, in sickness and in health; and do you pledge to love him (each other) so long as you both shall live?

"I Do"

Vow, Pledge or Promise 9: Pledge, Ring Exchange and Affirmation

I, Sylvia, declare that I love you, Tom, with an open and honest heart. I promise to cherish, comfort and support you and I willingly choose to live my life with you both freed and joined by love. This ring is a symbol of my love and commitment.

Sylvia places Tom's ring. Then, Tom makes his pledge and places Sylvia's ring. The Officiant confirms:

Do you, Sylvia, take Tom to be your lawfully wedded husband, to create a life with him in good times and in bad, in wealth and in poverty, in sickness and in health, so long as you both shall live?

"I Do"

Do you, Tom, take Sylvia . . .

"I Do"

In sharing this moment two become one. Each a part of the whole, individual and distinct, yet united in love and caring.

ADVANCED CURRICULUM FOR LOVERS: VOWS

Consider the promises you are about to make to your beloved. Think deeply about the values you intend to live by and the framework for the love you offer to each other. "Love, honor, respect…""…support, friendship, understanding…" "…for better or for worse…"

Are these also gifts you give yourself? Or, are you looking for qualities in your partner, and from your marriage that you are have not yet developed within you? What can you do or begin today to enhance your relationship with yourself?

"It is not only marrying the right person, it is being the right partner."

The Art of Marriage

Rings

Rings 1:

Officiant: The Ring symbolizes the continuous Circle of Eternal Life. This ring is a reminder of the love between Bernie and Elton. It is an outward visible sign of an inward spiritual unity. (Couple may exchange rings with or without additional statements)

Rings 2:

Clark-

Lois, I give you this ring as a sign of my vow, and with all that I am, and all that I have, I honor you.

Clark places Lois' ring, then Lois declares . . .

Rings 3:

We are gathered today in a circle of love and support around Elton and Bernie. And we hope these rings, circles of precious metal, may serve to remind you both of what is more precious still: the depth of love and understanding you have for each other, and of how that grows with respect during your circle of life together.

Rings 4:

With this ring, I thee wed.

I promise that from this day forward, you shall not walk alone.

My heart will be your shelter, and my arms will be your home.

May you feel deeply loved, for indeed you are.

I choose to go with you always as your beloved husband/wife/partner.

Rings 5:

One couple placed this Ring Blessing after the Prayer and before the Vows. Then they exchanged rings while making Pledges; and finally Affirmed their vows. See Vows, **V9**.

In many cultures, the circle is a symbol of wholeness. For Native

Americans that wholeness is made complete by embracing the diversity of the four directions and four elements. A circle also represents a journey—beginning, traveling through adventures and trials, then ending by returning to the same place it began, but with a perspective enriched and matured by the experiences along the way.

Percy and Mary begin and end life the same way: alone with their maker. And yet they do not return to that place unchanged, for each will bring the memories and lessons and love to be gathered during their journey. The rings being exchanged today are crafted of gold, one of the finest materials we humans can borrow from the Earth. Their physical beauty is but a shadow compared to what they represent.

Mary and Percy, you each began life alone with your God, and will end it the same way, but the preciousness of the memories you create together, the lessons you learn with and from each other, and the love you share will enrich your souls for all eternity. The true value of these rings, then, is to serve as a symbol of these riches which you will discover together. May your marriage support and embrace all you bring to it, just as we here today in this circle of friends and family support and embrace your commitment to each other and to your union.

And so we ask for a blessing upon these rings and upon the marriage they will represent. May they serve to remind Mary and Percy of their vows to one another, may your grace and presence be with them always.

Blessings

Blessing 1:

May you walk in the Light.

May you reflect the Power and Love of the Light.

May you find what you seek as you walk your path with one another.

Amen

Blessing 2:

Now you will feel no rain,

For each of you will be shelter to the other.

Now you will feel no cold,
For each of you will be warmth to the other.

Now there is no loneliness for you

Now you are two persons

But there is one life before you.

Go now to your dwelling place to enter into the days of your togetherness.

And may your days be good and long upon the earth.

Apache Wedding Blessing (apocryphal)

Blessing 3:

Splendor is upon everything

Blessing is upon everything

Who is full of this abundance

Bless this groom and bride.

Hebrew Blessing

Blessing 4:

Blessed are the man and the woman

who have grown beyond themselves

and have seen through their separations.

They delight in the way things are

and keep their hearts open, day and night.

They are like trees planted near flowing rivers,

which bear fruit when they are ready.

Their leaves will not fall or wither.

Everything they do will succeed.

Derived from The Book of Psalms, Psalm I:1-3

Blessing 5:

May George and Martha keep this covenant; may the inspiration of this hour remain with them. May they, trusting each other, trust life and may they continue to love each other forever. May the love, companionship, and friendliness of the home be an inspiration to family and loved ones.

or

George and Martha, may you keep this covenant; may the inspiration of this hour remain with you. May you, trusting each other, trust life and may you continue to love each other forever. May the love, companionship, and friendliness of your home be an inspiration to family and loved ones.

Blessing 6:

David and Bathsheba, teach your children the value of loving, for they learn from your example. Give your children the freedom to find their own way, and always stand by them. For children are the fulfillment of yesterdays dreams, the creation of today's joys and the hope for tomorrows future.

David and Bathsheba, may you encourage each other in whatever you set out to achieve. Together, may you discover a love that gives you the courage to stand together as companions, to face every challenge and enjoy every success.

Blessing 7:

Go into the world and hold fast to your ideals. Give one another new experiences of joy. You have come to this threshold in your lives because of your caring for and your commitment to each other. May this love now sealed with marriage mature and enrich the experiences of you both. May your home be bright with the laughter of family and friends. May it be a source of peace and strength for all who gather there.

Blessing 8:

The Lord bless you and keep you;

the Lord make his face to shine upon you,

and be gracious to you;

the Lord lift up his countenance upon you,

and give you peace.

Numbers 6:24–26

Blessing 9:

Therefore what God has joined together, let no man separate.

Matthew 19:6

Pronouncements

Pronouncement 1:

I believe in the power of your agreement today. I feel your love for each other and have faith in the seriousness with which you make this commitment.

May you go with God. May you walk in His Countenance. May you reflect His power and love. May you find what you seek as you walk down the path with one another. I now pronounce you husband and wife.

Pronouncement 2:

It is the creative, not the indulgent love which

refines our selfishness, deepens our personalities,

and make life more meaningful.

Harry and Bess, by exchanging vows and rings,

you have underscored your marriage to each other

in the presence of this gathering.

From here on, each of you will see your own experience in a

new light as your life together unfolds.

May you have the courage to love in each other,

and by implication, in others on this earth, the truth that is yet to be,

the truth that shall always be new.

Pronouncement 3:

Because Samson and Delilah have pledged their love and commitment to each other before these witness, I now pronounce them husband and wife.

Pronouncement 4:

As witnessed by your family and friends, it is my pleasure to pronounce you John, and you, Jackie, husband and wife, lovers and friends for life.

Will you honor each other with a kiss?

3. Words of Love

Special Poems and Prose

I have organized these wonderful Words to compliment the categories of the ceremony—Commencement, Heart and Conclusion—based upon my experience and sense of where they best serve to inspire. Feel free to ignore my suggestion for placement and go with your hearts and senses. Use them whole or in part, as you see fit. For example, the *Apache Wedding Blessing* serves well as a Blessing to follow the Ring Exchange. Whereas, quoting only the last two lines, spoken by the Officiant, creates finality that may suffice for Blessing and Pronouncement.

You will find other sources of appropriate prose and poetry in the library, on-line, and in the resource pages of this book.

Commencement: Preceding or following Opening Remarks, Statement, Invocation

Love alone is capable of uniting living beings in such a way as to complete and fulfill them, for it alone takes them and joins them by what is deepest in themselves.

Pierre Teilhard de Chardin

Love has no other desire but to fulfill itself.

But if you love and must needs have desires, let these be your desires:

To melt and be like a running brook that sings its melody to the night.

To know the pain of too much tenderness.

To be wounded by your own understanding of love;

And to bleed willingly and joyfully.

To wake at dawn with a winged hearty and give thanks for another day of loving;

To rest at the noon hour and meditate love's ecstasy;

To return home at eventide with gratitude;

And then to sleep with a prayer for the beloved in your heart and a song of praise upon your lips.

The Prophet (On Love)
Kahlil Gibran

In a time when nothing is more certain than change, the commitment of two people to one another has become difficult and rare. Yet, by its scarcity, the beauty and value of this exchange have only been enhanced.

"The Vow"
Robert Sexton

Life leads the thoughtful man on a path
of many windings.
Now the course is crooked, not it runs
straight again.
Here winged thoughts may pour freely forth in words,
There the heavy burden of knowledge must be
shut away in silence.
But when two people are at home in their inmost hearts,
They shatter even the strength of iron or of bronze.
And when two people understand each other
in their inmost hearts,
Their words are sweet and strong,
like the fragrance of orchids.

Confucius

From every human being there rises a light that reaches straight to
heaven. And when two souls that are destined to be together find each
other, their streams of light flow together, and a single brighter light goes
forth from their united being.

Ba'al Shem Tov

the quiet thoughts

of two people a long time in love

touch lightly

like birds nesting in each other' warmth

you will know them by their laughter

but to each other

they speak mostly through their solitude

if they find themselves apart

they may dream of sitting undisturbed

in each other's presence

of wrapping themselves warmly

in each other's easy

Notes on Love and Courage
Hugh Prather

(This is a wonderful piece to include in a program or in the forward to your guest-signing book)

Blessed are the man and the woman

who have grown beyond themselves

and have seen through their separations.

They delight in the way things are

and keep their hearts open, day and night.

They are like trees planted near flowing rivers,

which bear fruit when they are ready.

Their leaves will not fall or wither.

Everything they do will succeed.

Derived from The Book of Psalms, Psalm 1:1-3

Beloved,

Let us love one another

Because love is of God;

Everyone who loves is begotten of God

And has knowledge of God.

The man without love has known nothing of God,

For God is love.

Love, then, consists in this:

Not that we have loved God,

But that he has loved us.

If God has loved us so,

We must have the same love for one another.

No one has ever seen God.

Yet if we love one another

God dwells in us,

And his love is brought to perfection in us.

We have come to know and to believe in the love God has for us.

God is love,

And he who abides in love

Abides in God, and God in him

1 John 4:7-12; 16; 18-19

Jewish Seven Blessings

Blessed are You, God, who brings forth fruit from the vine.

Blessed are You, God, who shapes the universe.

Blessed are You, Holy One of blessing, who fashions each person.

We bless You, God, for forming each person in your image.

You have planted within us a vision of You and given us the means that we may flourish through time.

Blessed are You, Creator of humanity.

Rejoice and be glad you who have wandered homeless. In joy have you gathered with your sisters and brothers. Blessed is the joy of our gathering.

Let these loving friends taste the bliss You gave to the first man and woman in the garden of Eden.

Blessed are You, the Presence who dwells with bride and groom in delight.

Blessed are You, God, Source of the universe, who lights the world with happiness and contentment, love and companionship, peace and friendship, bridegroom and bride.

May we all see the day when the sounds of joy fill the streets of the world — the voice of the groom and the voice of the bride, the happy shouts of their friends and companions.

We bless You, God, who brings bride and groom together to rejoice in each other.

Heart: Following Prayer, before Vows or Ring Exchange

You were born together, and together you shall be forevermore.

Ay, you shall be together even in the silent memory of God.

But let there be spaces in your togetherness,

And let the winds of the heavens dance between you.

Love one another, but make not a bond of love:

Let it rather be a moving sea between the shores of your souls.

Fill each other's cup but drink not from one cup.

Give one another of your bread but eat not from the same loaf.

Sing and dance together and be yours, but let each one of you be alone,

Even as the strings of a lute are alone though they quiver with the same music.

Give your hearts, but not into each other's keeping.

For only the hand of life can contain your hearts.

And stand together yet not too near together:

For the pillars of the temple stand apart,

And the oak tree and the cypress grow not in each other's shadow.

The Prophet (On Marriage)
Kahlil Gibran

I want to love you without clutching, appreciate you without judging, join you without invading, invite you without demanding, leave you without guilt, criticize you without blaming, and help you without insulting, I if can have the same from you then we can truly meet and enrich each other.

Making Contact
Virginia Satir

I love you,
Not only for what you are
But for what I am
When I am with you.
I love you,
Not only for what
You have made of yourself
But for what
You are making of me.
I love you,
For the part of me
That you bring out;
I love you,
For putting your hand
Into my heaped-up heart
And passing over
All the foolish, weak things
That you can't help
Dimly seeing there,
And for drawing out
Into the light
All the beautiful belongings
That no one else had looked
Quite far enough to find.
I love you because you
are helping me to make
Of the lumber of my life
Not a tavern
But a temple;
Out of works
Of my every day
Not a reproach
But a song . . .

Roy Croft

You have become mine forever.
Yes, we have become partners.
I have become yours.
Hereafter, I cannot live without you.
Do not live without me.
Let us share the joys.
We are word and meaning, united.
You are thought and I am sound.
May the nights be honey-sweet for us.
May the mornings be honey-sweet for us.
May the plants be honey-sweet for us.
May the earth be honey-sweet for us.

Hindu Marriage Poem

Song by Allen Ginsberg

The weight of the world
is love.
Under the burden
of solitude,
under the burden
of dissatisfaction
the weight,
the weight we carry
is love
Who can deny?
In dreams
it touches the
the body,
in thought
constructs
a miracle,
in imagination
anguishes
'til born
in human—
looks out of the heart
burning with purity—
for the burden of life
is love,
but we carry the weight
wearily,
and so must rest
in the arms of love
at last,
must rest in the arms
of love.
No rest
without love,
no sleep
without dreams

of love—
be mad or chill
obsessed with angels
or machines,
the final wish
is love
—cannot be bitter,
cannot deny,
cannot withhold
if denied:
the weight is too heavy
—must give
for no return
as thought
is given
in solitude
in all the excellence
of its excess.
The warm bodies
shine together
in the darkness,
the hand moves
to the center
of the flesh,
the skin trembles
in happiness
and the soul comes
joyful to the eye—
yes, yes,
that's what
I wanted,
I always wanted,
I always wanted,
to return
to the body
where I was born.

Conclusion: Following Heart of the ceremony, to bring the ceremony to a graceful ending.

Now you will feel no rain,

For each of you will be shelter to the other.

Now you will feel no cold,
For each of you will be warmth to the other.

Now there is no loneliness for you

Now there is no more loneliness,

Now there is no more loneliness.
Now you are two persons

But there is one life before you.

Go now to your dwelling place to enter into the days of your togetherness.

And may your days be good and long upon the earth.

Apache Wedding Blessing (apocryphal)

Just as water reflects the face

So one human heart reflects another.

Proverbs 27:19

See Blessings section in Part I for additional ideas. As I have stated before, I think it is best to bring the ceremony to a swift and neat conclusion after you have declared your love and promises and exchanged rings. Why add another layer of icing to the cake?

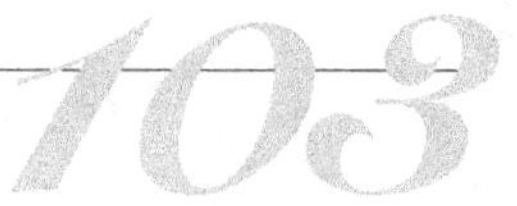

4 Civil Rites and Rituals

Rituals create ceremonies within ceremony. They can be the special touch needed to personalize your ceremony. Included with each ritual is a suggestion for placement within the ceremony, which you may ignore, of course.

Wine Ceremony

(Before or after the exchange of rings)

Wine is poured into the wine glass, Officiant offers the glass to the couple with a blessing—

Wine is the Symbol of Life (Vitality)

The flow within our bodies

Buy sharing this wine glass, two become one

A part of the whole, each separate,

Yet united in love.

(Each sips from the wine glass)

Bells or Tibetan Bowls

(Between Invocation and Vows, or just following Vows)

Officiant: The ringing of these bells is a symbol of Harmony. Each bowl's vibration is distinct, like the individual. But together a new resonance is created. The harmony created today will continue with them throughout their lives.

(Each strikes the bowl/bell simultaneously)

Breaking the Wine Glass

(Signals the end of ceremony; immediately after kiss)

The wine glass is wrapped in a heavy cloth, placed on the ground, and the groom stomps on it, shattering the glass. This signals the end of the ceremony and the beginning of festivities. Anyone who wishes may shout, "Mazel Tov!" (Congratulations). From Jewish tradition, whose contemporary symbolism lies in breaking with the past, breaking from the families of origin and the single life.

Water Ceremony

(Before or after exchange of rings)

A couple who met in the water (San Francisco Bay) decided to have a water sharing ceremony. Water may represent the emotional aspect, the feminine, purification, and, like the ocean, the source of all life on our planet.

Candle Lighting

(Before opening statements; prior to vows, between vows and rings)

The couple lights a candle together, or each lights a candle, or each arrives with a lit candle, which they then pass to a parent or a friend as they arrive at the circle.

Fire symbolizes illumination, light and warmth that draw us together, and the ability to cleanse and purify.

Honor thy Parents

(Beginning of ceremony at close of procession; key readings in ceremony)

Many couples choose to acknowledge and honor their parents as the ceremony commences. Making special statements and giving gifts are ways to show gratitude for your upbringing and to demonstrate your love.

Some couples carry a single **rose or a small gift** to the altar or circle. As the bride joins her groom, each turns to his own parents to present a rose or gift.

Many couples give their parents a **kiss** before they complete their procession to the Officiant.

Some choose to make a **special statement**. See the Special Statements section for examples of readings from a bride and groom to their respective parents. Here's a short and sweet example:

Officiant points out parents to the guests—

"We would like to take a moment to honor the parents of Florence—William and Doris; and the parents of Antony—Ainslie and Pax. These parents have deeply touched the lives of their children; these children are blessed and grateful for the support and love of their parents."

Another way to honor the parents is to ask them to provide a special **reading, song, poem or blessing** during the ceremony.

If for some reason, such as divorce or separation of the parents, the parents do not wish to be prominent in the ceremony, you might ask one or two of them to **witness your marriage license**.

Exchanging Roses, Gifts, Special Statements or Stories

(Entering into the Heart of the ceremony, before Vows)

You and your partner may exchange **roses** of a color symbolizing your love, devotion, purity, fidelity.

You may exchange **bread** or **cake** as a symbol of home and hearth, abundance, grace.

You may wish to **tell a story** (short) about how you met, or how you fell in love; the endearing qualities or quirky traits unique to your lover; what marriage and partnership mean to you . . .

Casting a Circle

(Brief casting may be done at close of Processional; just prior to Vows)

Casting a circle is an ancient Pagan ritual. It is appropriate to think of it as designating a sacred space—a healing space, where agreements can be made or broken, where powerful recognitions happen.

Within the circle, time stops. The circle is the ultimate representation of eternity within flowing time; present time, no time.

Circles of flower petals or stones may be placed before the processional, so you can step into the pre-formed circle. Or, you may assign someone to cast the circle around you as the commencement ritual.

A simple explanatory statement may accompany the casting:

Clark and Lois, you stand at the center of the Circle where all things meet their opposites: Male and Female; Darkness and Light; Spirit and Matter; God and Goddess; That which make each whole and complete; Just as you two are about to join as one.

Smudging or Purifying

(At the entrance to the celebration area, or at the close of processional with all assembled)

In some American Indian tribes, important meetings and gatherings begin with purifying rituals. "Smudging" with smoke or incense is a ritual that enables people to clarify and purify their energy field. Smoke symbolizes the pure spirit, the sacred space, prayers rising to God.

Typically, bundles of dried white or purple sage are burned in a bowl or shell. Smoke from the sage is inhaled and "brushed" over the body to cleanse the aura, and assist the smudgee to release energy, thoughts or feelings that might interfere with being fully present.

Have a close friend or relative light the sage and walk the bowl around to the people who wish to be smudged. Even people who aren't "religious or spiritual" report feeling calmed and brought into a quiet space by the sage smoke.

Build an Altar

(If elaborate or private, build before the ceremony; if a simple design, assemble between Invocation and Prayer; ask participating guests to bring a sacred object or gift)

Think about who you are as spirit, how you were raised and your spiritual beliefs and practices. Bring together a small assortment of objects, statuary, fruit and grains, mementos, photos, etc. Candles, fabric, plants or wood, metal, and water help to bring in the Earth elements. Place the objects on a small table or designated area. You may offer private prayers at your altar.

Calling the Four Directions

(Early in ceremony; following Statement, in place of Invocation)

Inspired by Lakota tribal custom and medicine, the Four Directions refers to the Four Powers of the Medicine Wheel. A wedding wheel may be constructed to encircle the couple, the wedding party, or the entire group of attendees, while the powers of the four directions are called into the circle.

The four powers are symbolized aspects of nature as well as qualities of character that a person must develop over a lifetime to become Whole. The information below shows you the direction, quality, animal totem, and color associated with each direction. I have included suggestions for 'gifts' for the earth powers that you call into the circle, as well as the order in which they are invoked.

South Innocence   Mouse Green (green feather, fresh sage, seeds)

East   Illumination Eagle   Yellow   (corn, squash, seeds, candle)

North Wisdom   Buffalo White   (white feather, white corn)

West   Introspection Bear   Black   (tobacco, black feather, beads)

Smudging (see above) may be included with calling on the Four Powers, or honoring the Four Directions. As the shaman or officiant calls in the directions, a 'smudge bowl' may be walked around the wheel, smoke brushed along the borders and points.

At each point, the shaman or officiant invokes the spirit from that direction, clears the point with incense, and places a sacred object or gift to mark the direction.

Facing the south perimeter, smudge to clear:

"Facing South; we invoke the Mouse spirit and welcome its gift of Innocence to our hearts."

Places a gift to mark the point, then walks to the right, to the east point, smudges:

"Recognizing East; we invoke the Eagle spirit and welcome its gift of illumination with our whole being."

Places a gift to mark the point, then walks to the right, to the north point, smudges:

"Acknowledging North; we invoke the Buffalo spirit and welcome Wisdom into our minds."

Places a gift to mark the point, then walks to the right, to the west point, smudges:

"Moving West; we invoke the Bear spirit and welcome the opportunity to turn within."

Handfasting

(Applied before the Vows, loosed for the ring exchange)

The couples join hands. The Officiant drapes a cord or ribbon over their wrists. It is customary to tie a lover's knot, but failing that knowledge, I have performed the task by looping the ends of the cords around the wrists from opposite sides.

"Now as I tie this true Lover's Knot you two are joined as one. Gentle are the bonds of this union. Pull one way the bonds are strengthened. Pull the other and they are loosened. Keep this knot as a token of your spiritual bonds."

Anointing with Oil or Water

(Just prior to vows, as a prayer and preparation; in place of the Invocation)

Z Budapest, a Wicce priestess, offers these rituals to purify and prepare the couple for their new relationship.

Using a natural oil, with essential oil (scent) added for special symbolic significance, the Officiant touches a drop of oil (water) to

Forehead	I purify you from all anxiety
	I purify your mind from fears
Eyes	I purify your eyes to see Her ways
Lips	I purify your lips to speak Her names
Breast	I purify your breast formed in strength and beauty
Genitals	Your genitals I bless for strength and pleasure
Feet	Your feet I bless to walk in Her path

I invoke you, Goddess of All Life, I invoke you by the foods here present, by the roots to make a strong foundation for this relationship, by the stems for standing firm and proud, by the leaves to grow and prosper together, by the flowers for joy and laughter, and by the fruits for a long and prosperous time together.

Natural Essential Oils are water soluble (non-staining) essence of plants, roots and trees. They may be added to water or oil, or salt. Some are available as incense. May I suggest—

Inspiration: Clary Sage, Sandalwood, Rosemary, Lavender

Sacredness: Frankincense, Basil, Amber, Rose

Balance: Clary Sage, Neroli, Rose, Rosewood

Love: Rose, Musk, Ylang-Ylang, Ginseng, Bergamot

Joy: Rose, Bergamot, Ylang-Ylang, Neroli, Blood Orange, Mint

Practically Perfect
Wedding
and
Commitment
Ceremonies:
Bibliography
and Resources

Your Complete Wedding Planner for the perfect bride and groom to be
Marjabelle Young Stewart
1989   St. Martins Press, NY
Primarily etiquette; traditional weddings, no ceremony information; defers to
traditional religious clergy for ceremony details.

Lesbian and Gay Marriage: Private Commitments, Public Ceremonies
Edited by Suzanne Sherman
1992   Temple University Press
No ceremony texts; experiences and opinions on religion and modern love and
commitment; Universal Life Ministries officiations; resource directory and good
reading list.

On Writing Well: The Classic Guide to Writing Nonfiction
William Zinsser
1976   HarperCollins Publishers
Interesting and timeless, an "easy read" for basics of well constructed language
and text.

I Do: A guide to creating you own unique wedding ceremony
Sydney Barbara Metrick
1992   Celestial Arts Publishing, Berkeley
Well-researched little book of rituals, planning tips and ceremonies punctuated
with historical information on the origins of the tradition.

Weddings by Design: A guide to the non-traditional ceremony
Richard Leviton
1993   Harper San Francisco/Harper Collins Publishers
A royal banquet of ceremonial history and traditions from all over the world.

The Prophet
Kahlil Gibran
1923   Alfred A Knopf, Inc. (1961), NYC
Exquisite poetry; spiritually and intellectually provocative.

The Holy Book of Women's Mysteries
Z Budapest
1989   Wingbow Press, Berkeley, California
(pp. 88-89); chock full of modern witch and pagan ritual and belief.
www.zbudapest.com also c/o Woman's Spirituality Forum, Oakland, California

Seven Arrows
Hyemeyohsts Storm
1972   Ballantine Books
American Indian culture and customs and spiritual traditions woven into the
"great story" of the people.

Words for the Wedding: Perfect things to say for a perfect wedding day
Wendy Paris and Andrew Chesler
2001   Perigee/Putnam Penquin Books
"Creative ideas for choosing and using hundreds of quotations to personalize
your vows, toasts, invitations and more."

*The Spirit of Loving: Reflections on love and relationship by writers, psychotherapists
and spiritual teachers.*
edited by Emily Hilburn Sell
1995   Shambhala Publications, Boston

Undefended Love
Jett Psaris, Ph.D., Marlena S. Lyons, Ph.D.
2000   New Harbinger Publications, Inc., Berkeley
Wisdom and experience on love and intimacy from the co-founders of the
Conscious Living Center in S.F. Bay Area.

Spiritual Literacy: Reading the sacred in everyday life
Frederic and Mary Ann Brussat
1996   Touchstone, NYC
Wonderful compendium of spiritual prose and poetry from every tradition,
every age.

*Weddings from the Heart: Contemporary and Traditional Ceremonies for an
Unforgettable Wedding*
Daphne Rose Kingma
1991   Conari Press, Berkeley, California
Wonderful prose, great ideas and personal touches

Sacred Contracts: Awakening your Divine Potential
Carolyn Myss, PhD
2002   Three Rivers Press, New York
Deep resource for deeper self-understanding

Anatomy of the Spirit: The Seven Stages of Healing
Caroline Myss, PhD
1996   Harmony Books, New York
A must for spiritual delvers and energy healers

Web sites, www.:

theknot.com

google: atheists.org or atheistwedding

About the Author

Angel Booth is a teaching minister and writer living in Northern California. She is a graduate of the seminary of Church of Natural Grace in San Francisco, where she taught meditation, healing and intuition development for 17 years. Since 1989 she has officiated marriages, partnership ceremonies, baptisms, memorials, life transitions, healings and blessings.

With her experience and reservoir of ceremony material, Angel assists people to create the perfect ceremony, tailored for personality, beliefs and lifestyle values.

Angel offers private and group instruction in meditation and guided imagery, mentoring for spiritual practice, and coaching from a spiritual perspective.

For information, questions, corrections or attributions regarding this book, please contact Angel Booth at 29angels@gmail.com

Church of Natural Grace and its meditation school, Psychic Horizons, may be contacted directly for inspiring meditation services, classes, energy healings and readings.

Church of Natural Grace/Psychic Horizons
972 Valencia Street
San Francisco, CA 94110
415 643-8800

www.ingramcontent.com/pod-product-compliance
Lightning Source LLC
Chambersburg PA
CBHW060201120726
48004CB00007B/1637

9 798889 121894